Primary health and values

Written with

Jenni Harrold

www.prim-ed.com

Other titles to support this curriculum area

Copymasters

Bullying • Conflict Resolution • Lifestyle Choices • Don't Sit! Get Fit!
Self-esteem • Values Education • Transition Issues

Other Books

Dino-might Bullying Readers

Posters

Bullying • Dino-might Bullying • Conflict Resolution
Lifestyle Choices • Self-esteem • Values

0579C

Primary health and values–Book F
Prim-Ed Publishing.

Published in 2006 by Prim-Ed Publishing.
Reprinted under licence by Prim-Ed Publishing, 2006.
Copyright Jenni Harrold and R.I.C. Publications 2003
*The author wishes to acknowledge the extensive
knowledge of the writers at R.I.C. Publications who
contributed to this project.*

This master may only be reproduced by the original
purchaser for use with their class(es). The publisher
prohibits the loaning or onselling of this master for the
purposes of reproduction.

ISBN 1 84654 045 3
PR–0579

Additional titles available in this series:
Primary health and values–Book A
Primary health and values–Book B
Primary health and values–Book C
Primary health and values–Book D
Primary health and values–Book E
Primary health and values–Book G

View all pages online.

Email Address: sales@prim-ed.com
Home Page: http://www.prim-ed.com

Internet websites
In some cases, websites or specific URLs may be recommended. While these are checked and rechecked at the time of publication,
the publisher has no control over any subsequent changes which may be made to webpages. It is *strongly* recommended that the
class teacher checks *all* URLs before allowing students to access them.

Primary health and values

Foreword

Primary health and values introduces and develops the knowledge, skills, attitudes and values that will assist pupils to lead healthy and fulfilling lives. Pupils will consider what it means to be healthy–physically, socially, mentally and emotionally–and will be given experiences to assist them to become responsible, caring members of society.

The book is divided into two sections. The first section–**Healthy lifestyles**–offers pupils the knowledge to make informed decisions about safety, nutrition, the media, drugs and more. Through guided classroom discussions and activities, pupils are encouraged to think critically about health issues and the challenges they face as they grow and develop.

The second section–**Personal development and relationships**–focuses on character building and values. Most experts agree that people with defined values and a good self-image are better equipped to deal with challenging situations. The activities in this section encourage pupils to consider their own values and develop a sense of self-worth. This section also focuses on the importance of showing respect for and tolerance towards others and valuing diversity in our society.

Primary health and values provides coverage of the health curriculum, supports teachers in planning and implementing lessons and, through collaborative learning and thoughtful discussion, promotes a lifelong commitment to healthy, active lifestyles.

Other titles in this series:

Primary health and values – Book A

Primary health and values – Book B

Primary health and values – Book C

Primary health and values – Book D

Primary health and values – Book E

Primary health and values – Book G

Contents

Primary health and values is divided into two sections. These are:

Healthy lifestyles – offers pupils the knowledge to make informed decisions about safety, nutrition, exercise, the media, drugs and more. Through guided classroom discussions and activities, pupils are encouraged to think critically about health issues and the challenges they face as they grow and develop.

Personal development and relationships – focuses on character building and values. The activities in this section encourage pupils to consider their own values and develop a sense of self-worth. This section also focuses on the importance of showing respect and tolerance towards others and valuing diversity in our society.

The notes on the following pages provide comprehensive information about terms and concepts used in this book.

A teachers page accompanies each pupil worksheet. It provides the following information:

Background information has been included to enhance the teacher's understanding of the concept being taught and to provide additional information to relate to the pupils.

Specific objectives explain what the pupils are expected to demonstrate through completing the activities.

Discussion points have been suggested to further develop ideas on the pupil worksheet. They can also encourage the pupils to comprehend, assess and form opinions about what they have read.

What to do gives suggested step-by-step instructions for the activity. The accompanying worksheet may be the focus of the activity or it may be where the pupils record their ideas after completing a task or discussion.

Answers to all worksheet activities are included. Some answers will need a teacher check, while others will vary depending on the pupils' personal experiences, opinions etc.

Additional activities can be used to further develop the objectives being assessed. These activities provide ideas to consolidate and clarify the concepts and skills taught in the activity.

Curriculum links appropriate to each country are provided across the main learning area.

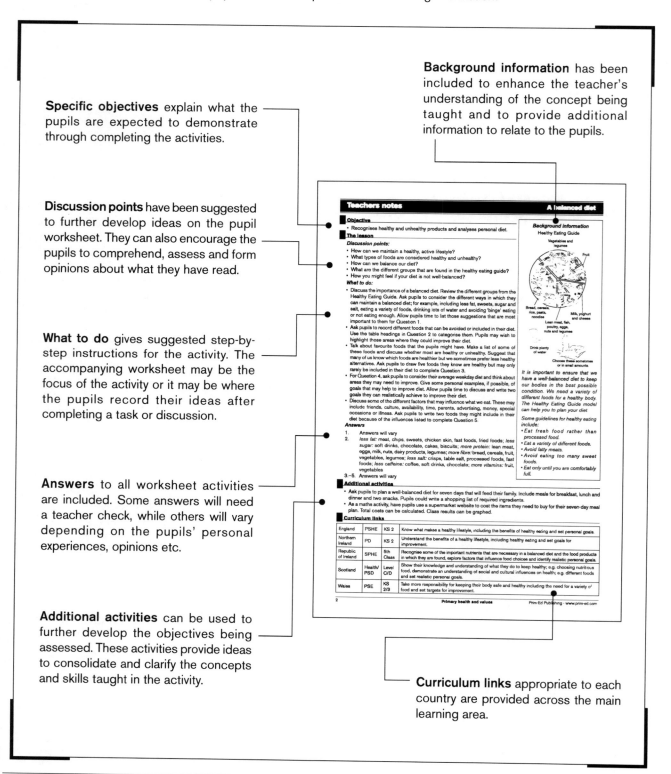

A variety of pupil worksheets are provided, which may contain a selection of role-plays to perform; scenarios to read and consider; information to read, discuss and answer questions about; or values or feelings to consider and compare with others.

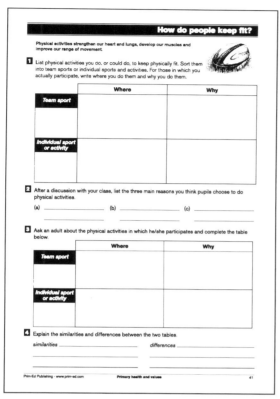

Pupil activities to reinforce and develop understanding of the concept.

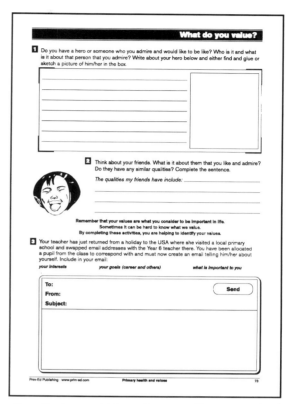

Questioning activities where pupils are required to consider and evaluate personal feelings or values.

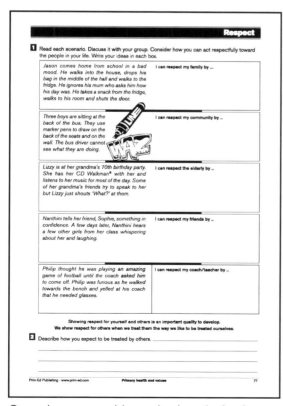

Several pages provide a selection of role-plays or scenarios for pupils to use in a variety of ways.

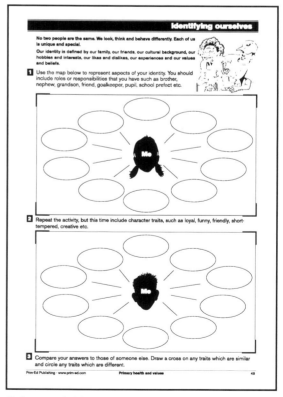

Other activities include completing tables or reading and labelling diagrams.

Primary health and values introduces and develops the knowledge, skills, attitudes and values that will enable pupils to lead healthy and fulfilling lives. Pupils will consider what it means to be healthy—physically, socially, mentally and emotionally—and will be given the tools to become responsible, caring members of society.

Many of the activities in this book provide pupils with an opportunity to formulate their thoughts on a topic and express their opinions and feelings. Classroom discussions are valuable for encouraging critical and reflective thinking.

Teaching health

- Create a safe atmosphere in the classroom so pupils feel they can share their thoughts and feelings.

- Identify what it is the pupils are going to take away from the lesson. (Refer to the 'Objective' in the Teachers notes for each activity.)

- Begin with a discussion or, with older pupils, a hypothetical situation. (Refer to the 'Discussion points' in the Teachers notes for each activity.)

- Listen to and be honest with the pupils. (Give something of yourself. Share some of your own experiences, where appropriate.)

- Show respect for the pupils' thoughts and feelings.

- Be non-judgmental.

In your responses, encourage pupils to analyse their statements by asking such things as 'What could happen if you did that?' or 'Who else would be affected by that?', rather than giving your own opinion.

With some topics, pupils may make suggestions where you can respond 'Is that the RIGHT thing to do?'. Such a question can promote discussions regarding individual, group, community and global values. Who is it 'right' for?

Although pupils should feel free to express their opinions, it is important that they understand there is a 'right' conclusion, rather than letting them think whatever they conclude is correct.

Creating a safe atmosphere

For an effective health lesson to take place, pupils need to feel comfortable enough to share their thoughts, feelings, opinions and past experiences. They need to feel there will be no ridicule, no put-downs and a non-judgmental atmosphere.

One way to promote this safe atmosphere during discussions with younger pupils is to make the effort to sit the pupils in a circle, even if it means going to another room to do this. Some schools call this time 'circle time'. Set clear rules, such as one pupil speaking at a time and no put-downs or pulling faces. Make the circle a 'safe place' where the pupils feel comfortable to talk openly about their feelings, worries and achievements.

Pupils can be encouraged to become respectful listeners. Ensure that pupils raise their hands if they wish to make a comment; or, for younger pupils, an item can be placed in the middle of the circle such as a 'talking stick' or small toy. Only pupils holding this are able to speak.

Explain to the class that many people only 'half listen' as they are thinking about what they might say when the speaker stops. Some people don't even wait for the speaker to stop, and interrupt him or her in the middle of a sentence. During 'circle time', teachers and pupils have the opportunity to share their thoughts without being interrupted.

It is important for pupils to understand that personal issues discussed during these 'open forum' meetings are not to become topics of conversation outside the classroom. Teachers will also need to show respect to the pupils unless, of course, issues are raised involving abuse or that need attention by parents. Teachers will then need to consult their headteachers/principals regarding any action that needs to be taken.

Once the class has a routine set in place to discuss health issues openly and respectfully, these skills can be transferred to discussions about issues affecting the class, such as conflict and bullying.

Growth and development/Drug education

The community is generally united in its overall opinions and goals in relation to young people. In the areas of growth and development and drug education, the form and timing of this education vary among different community groups and are based on a wide range of factors, mainly concerned with religious and community expectations.

Activities in both these areas are provided in this series; however, the author recognises the right of schools, teachers and parents to guide education according to their own priorities.

Values education

Most definitions agree that 'values' are those qualities which an individual or a society considers to be important as principles for conduct.

The *Primary health and values* series helps pupils to consider their personal strengths and weaknesses and reinforces the advantages of having a strong set of values.

A person's set of values affects his or her thinking and behaviour. When people are confident in themselves and have strong values, it is easier to do things that are 'right'. Those who have weaker values can often be led easily and may do things they don't really want to do.

Teachers can encourage pupils to have a positive self-image through praise and by recognising their achievements.

Teachers can foster the development of personal qualities such as perseverance, kindness and dealing with stress and criticism. They can also discuss some values with pupils, such as honesty, generosity and tolerance. Teachers might also like to discuss other things people may value, like pets, music and the environment.

Tolerance and empathy

Tolerance and empathy should be encouraged in pupils. Activities such as drama games, which require pupils to put themselves in someone else's place and imagine how that person feels, can help to foster empathy. Tolerance is an ongoing process that teaches pupils not to hate. Teachers can teach tolerance most effectively by modelling tolerant behaviour in the classroom and playground, ensuring pupils are exposed to multicultural literature and images, and teaching them about various faiths, ethnicity and lifestyles. Educating pupils to be tolerant will:

- promote the understanding and acceptance of individual differences,

- promote the idea that differences can enhance our relationships and enrich our society,

- minimise generalisations and stereotyping, and

- promote the need to combat prejudice and discrimination.

This book emphasises the importance of respecting the feelings and emotions of others. It uses scenarios to help pupils 'put themselves in the shoes' of others. When pupils develop empathy for others, the dynamics of situations can change.

Collaborative learning

When pupils are able to work together in groups, they are encouraged to communicate and express their ideas. It is important that teachers monitor groups working independently to ensure that all pupils are working together as a team. By allocating a role for each group member, it is more likely that the dynamics will be equitable. The roles of the pupils can be swapped regularly to give each member the opportunity to participate in all tasks.

Allow time at the end of the group tasks for the pupils to evaluate their team skills and to make targets to work towards the next time they form as a group. Some activities may work better if the groups are organised by ability levels, others will be enriched by mixed ability groupings. To enable all pupils to work together at some stage during the year, randomly select groups for some activities.

Differentiating activities

The activities in the *Primary health and values* series have been designed so they can be followed precisely or adapted by teachers. This flexibility allows teachers the opportunity to modify lessons and worksheets to meet the needs of pupils with varying abilities and special needs.

To meet the special needs of English as a second language (ESL) pupils or those who have low levels of literacy, plan a time to introduce keywords and concepts. Having other adult support is ideal as the group can work in a quiet area away from the classroom. Keywords can be enlarged and discussed. Being immersed in the language before a topic begins gives these pupils an advantage, especially during the teacher discussion part of the lesson when most teachers tend to speak quite quickly.

If other adults are not available, mixed ability groups will allow ESL pupils and pupils with low literacy levels to observe and be guided by other pupils.

Pupils who seem to 'race' through the activities and worksheets and who understand the content very quickly can be challenged by looking at the topic in greater depth (rather than being given more of the same). They can go beyond the facts and conduct research related to strands of the topics that interest them.

By meeting the needs of individual pupils, allowing the pupils to learn collaboratively and by having very clear instructions and expectations, health lessons should run smoothly.

Assessment

Below are the activity objectives from the activity pages of *Primary health and values* – Book F. These objectives can be transferred across to the assessment proforma on page x. The format of each proforma is ideal for inclusion in pupil portfolios or for reporting purposes. Using proformas allows teachers to provide a well explained, logically presented indication of progress to both pupils and parents.

Healthy lifestyles

Pages 2 – 3	• Recognises healthy and unhealthy products and analyses personal diet.
Pages 4 – 5	• Recognises factors essential for creating a balanced lifestyle.
Pages 6 – 7	• Understands that puberty is a time of change and that various factors can affect development for individuals.
Pages 8 – 9	• Describes ways of coping with changes that occur during puberty.
Pages 10 – 11	• Describes aspects of social and emotional growth and development.
Pages 12 – 13	• Recognises that changes occur in a consistent pattern although individuals are all unique.
Pages 14 – 15	• Identifies the effects of various substances on the body.
Pages 16 – 17	• Recognises that although cigarettes and alcohol are legal drugs, there are health and social risks associated with their use.
Pages 18 – 19	• Predicts and reflects in role-play situations on decisions to refuse cigarettes and alcohol.
Pages 20 – 21	• Recognises factors that influence participation in physical activities and the risks associated with a sedentary lifestyle.

Pages 22 – 23	• Identifies aspects of the environment that may prove unsafe.
Pages 24 – 25	• Recognises emergency situations and how to deal with them.
Pages 26 – 27	• Recognises influences on safe behaviour and the use of safety equipment.
Pages 28 – 29	• Recognises that there are different factors which influence our choice of health products and services.
Pages 30 – 31	• Recognises that different factors influence decisions regarding food selection.
Pages 32 – 33	• Understands that media images may not always promote a realistic representation.
Pages 34 – 35	• Recognises positive and negative influences of peers on behaviour.
Pages 36 – 37	• Makes judgments on the reliability of advertisements.
Pages 38 – 39	• Describes actions required to address a specific personal health issue.
Pages 40 – 41	• Identifies ways in which people stay fit.
	• Recognises factors that influence people's choices of participation in activities to stay fit.

Personal development and relationships

Pages 42 – 43	• Recognises personal feelings related to given statements.
Pages 44 – 45	• Understands the terms 'role' and 'responsibilities'.
	• Identifies own roles and responsibilities within different groups.
	• Comments on how he/she carries out each role and suggests personal improvements.
Pages 46 – 47	• Participates in teamwork activities requiring cooperation and communication.
	• Identifies the qualities of good teamwork.
	• Evaluates teamwork performance of his/her group.
Pages 48 – 49	• Completes an identity map about himself/herself.
Pages 50 – 51	• Selects strategies to develop self-esteem.
	• Writes positive statements or words about himself/herself.
	• Compares descriptions about himself/herself.

Pages 52 – 53	• Understands the meaning of the term 'stereotype'.
	• Identifies and describes stereotypes in real life and on television.
	• Realises the way people are treated according to a stereotype can affect their self-concept.
Pages 54 – 55	• Identifies and categorises scenarios into those that are bullying and those that are not.
Pages 56 – 57	• Considers the positive and negative effects peer pressure has on influencing behaviour and self-concept.
Pages 58 – 59	• Reviews current and past friendships.
	• Evaluates himself/herself as a person in order to develop friendships.
	• Establishes strategies to make new friendships while maintaining existing friendships.

Assessment

Pages 60 – 61	• Explores different types of relationships: child/parent, child/teacher, child/child.
	• Identifies different standards of behaviour in different relationships.
	• Identifies the expectations placed on him/her in different relationships.
Pages 62 – 63	• Uses conflict resolution steps to find solutions to scenarios.
Pages 64 – 65	• Identifies events that cause stress.
	• Identifies activities that aid relaxation.
	• Completes an action plan to combat stress.
	• Recognises a simple time management strategy.
Pages 66 – 67	• Follows decision-making steps to make a decision.
Pages 68 – 69	• Completes questions about empathy.
	• Interviews another pupil to gain some understanding of his/her feelings, attitudes, likes and dislikes.
Pages 70 – 71	• Identifies factors which make up a healthy or unhealthy lifestyle.

Pages 72 – 73	• Understands the meaning of values.
	• Identifies some of his/her own values.
Pages 74 – 75	• Identifies and describes tolerant and intolerant behaviour.
Pages 76 – 77	• Recognises actions that are disrespectful.
	• Considers ways to act respectfully toward others.
	• Identifies ways of showing respect to other people.
Pages 78 – 79	• Generates personal goals which are based on being fit and active.
	• Devises strategies to attain his/her personal goals.
	• Evaluates his/her decisions in the process of setting personal goals.
Pages 80 – 81	• Understands that commitment to a project is part of being responsible.
	• Considers carefully a project he/she would like to participate in and plans his/her involvement in detail.

Using the health and values assessment proforma (page x)

An explanation of how to use the proforma.

Learning area
• Fill in the appropriate learning area; for example, Health – Healthy lifestyles.

Task(s)
• Give a brief description of the activity and what was expected of the pupils.

Activity objective(s)
• Write the relevant objective(s) that match the activity (see the Teachers notes accompanying each worksheet).

Assessment
• Write the relevant curriculum objective(s) as listed on the teachers notes and assess appropriately.

Teacher comment
• Use this space to comment on aspects of an individual pupil's performance which cannot be indicated in the formal assessment, such as work habits or particular needs or abilities.

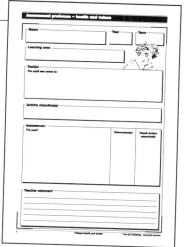

Using the skills and attitudes assessment proforma (page xi)

An explanation of how to use the proforma.

Assessment
• Assess the specific development of an individual pupil in these areas.

Teacher comment
• Use this space to comment on an individual pupil's skills and attitudes.

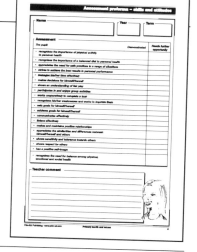

Name

Year

Term

Learning area

Task(s)

The pupil was asked to:

Activity objective(s)

Assessment

The pupil:

	Demonstrated	*Needs further opportunity*

Teacher comment

Assessment proforma – skills and attitudes

Name

Year

Term

Assessment

The pupil:	Demonstrated	Needs further opportunity
• recognises the importance of physical activity to personal health		
• recognises the importance of a balanced diet to personal health		
• appreciates the need for safe practices in a range of situations		
• strives to achieve the best results in personal performance		
• manages his/her time effectively		
• makes decisions for himself/herself		
• shows an understanding of fair play		
• participates in and enjoys group activities		
• works cooperatively to complete a task		
• recognises his/her weaknesses and works to improve them		
• sets goals for himself/herself		
• achieves goals for himself/herself		
• communicates effectively		
• listens effectively		
• makes and maintains positive relationships		
• appreciates the similarities and differences between himself/herself and others		
• shows sensitivity and tolerance towards others		
• shows respect for others		
• has a positive self-image		
• recognises the need for balance among physical, emotional and social health		

Teacher comment

Objective

- Recognises healthy and unhealthy products and analyses personal diet.

The lesson

Discussion points:

- How can we maintain a healthy, active lifestyle?
- What types of foods are considered healthy and unhealthy?
- How can we balance our diet?
- What are the different groups that are found in the healthy eating guide?
- How might you feel if your diet is not well-balanced?

What to do:

- Discuss the importance of a balanced diet. Review the different groups from the Healthy Eating Guide. Ask pupils to consider the different ways in which they can maintain a balanced diet; for example, including less fat, sweets, sugar and salt, eating a variety of foods, drinking lots of water and avoiding 'binge' eating or not eating enough. Allow pupils time to list those suggestions that are most important to them for Question 1.
- Ask pupils to record different foods that can be avoided or included in their diet. Use the table headings in Question 2 to categorise them. Pupils may wish to highlight those areas where they could improve their diet.
- Talk about favourite foods that the pupils might have. Make a list of some of these foods and discuss whether most are healthy or unhealthy. Suggest that many of us know which foods are healthier but we sometimes prefer less healthy alternatives. Ask pupils to draw five foods they know are healthy but may only rarely be included in their diet to complete Question 3.
- For Question 4, ask pupils to consider their average weekday diet and think about areas they may need to improve. Give some personal examples, if possible, of goals that may help to improve diet. Allow pupils time to discuss and write two goals they can realistically achieve to improve their diet.
- Discuss some of the different factors that may influence what we eat. These may include friends, culture, availability, time, parents, advertising, money, special occasions or illness. Ask pupils to write two foods they might include in their diet because of the influences listed to complete Question 5.

Answers

1. Answers will vary
2. *less fat:* meat, chips, sweets, chicken skin, fast foods, fried foods; *less sugar:* soft drinks, chocolate, cakes, biscuits; *more protein:* lean meat, eggs, milk, nuts, dairy products, legumes; *more fibre:* bread, cereals, fruit, vegetables, legumes; *less salt:* crisps, table salt, processed foods, fast foods; *less caffeine:* coffee, soft drinks, chocolate; *more vitamins:* fruit, vegetables
3.–5. Answers will vary

Background information

Healthy Eating Guide

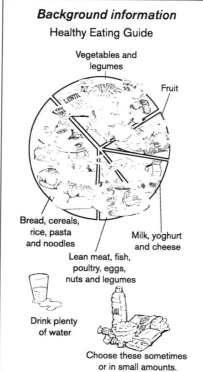

Vegetables and legumes

Fruit

Bread, cereals, rice, pasta and noodles

Milk, yoghurt and cheese

Lean meat, fish, poultry, eggs, nuts and legumes

Drink plenty of water

Choose these sometimes or in small amounts.

It is important to ensure that we have a well-balanced diet to keep our bodies in the best possible condition. We need a variety of different foods for a healthy body. The Healthy Eating Guide model can help you to plan your diet.

Some guidelines for healthy eating include:
- *Eat fresh food rather than processed food.*
- *Eat a variety of different foods.*
- *Avoid fatty meats.*
- *Avoid eating too many sweet foods.*
- *Eat only until you are comfortably full.*

Additional activities

- Ask pupils to plan a well-balanced diet for seven days that will feed their family. Include meals for breakfast, lunch and dinner and two snacks. Pupils could write a shopping list of required ingredients.
- As a maths activity, have pupils use a supermarket website to cost the items they need to buy for their seven-day meal plan. Total costs can be calculated. Class results can be graphed.

Curriculum links

England	PSHE	KS 2	Know what makes a healthy lifestyle, including the benefits of healthy eating and set personal goals.
Northern Ireland	PD	KS 2	Understand the benefits of a healthy lifestyle, including healthy eating and set goals for improvement.
Republic of Ireland	SPHE	5th Class	Recognise some of the important nutrients that are necessary in a balanced diet and the food products in which they are found, explore factors that influence food choices and identify realistic personal goals.
Scotland	Health/ PSD	Level C/D	Show their knowledge and understanding of what they do to keep healthy; e.g. choosing nutritious food, demonstrate an understanding of social and cultural influences on health; e.g. different foods and set realistic personal goals.
Wales	PSE	KS 2	Take more responsibility for keeping their body safe and healthy, including the need for a variety of food and set targets for improvement.

1 Make a list of the ways you can maintain a balanced diet.

_____

_____

2 Most of us can improve our diet in one or more ways. Write the foods to avoid or include.

less fat	
less sugar	
more protein	
more fibre	
less salt	
less caffeine	
more vitamins	

3 Draw five foods you know are healthy but you rarely include in your regular diet.

4 Consider your regular weekday diet. Write two goals that could help you to improve your diet and ensure it is more balanced.

5 There are many things that influence what we eat. Write two foods that you might include because of the following influences.

friends

_____

advertising

_____

parents

_____

culture

_____

Objective

• Recognises factors essential for creating a balanced lifestyle.

The lesson

Discussion points:

• What are the benefits of a healthy lifestyle?
• What areas of our lives do we need to focus on to maintain a balanced and healthy lifestyle?
• Why is it important to keep our minds healthy?
• What things make you feel happy and healthy?
• How can you balance your life?
• How much sleep do you usually get? Does that change on a weekend?
• What is mental health?

What to do:

• Discuss the different factors that are required to create a well-balanced lifestyle. If possible, the teacher could relate personal experiences and then ask pupils to volunteer examples of the different factors discussed. Discuss the importance of good mental health and what it means. Look at issues such as a positive outlook, being able to deal with stress and anxiety, feeling good about yourself, feeling depressed or unhappy and talking over problems and worries. Allow pupils time to complete the profile for Question 1.

• Ensure pupils understand that most people are not always able to keep a perfectly well-balanced lifestyle. There are always issues to be dealt with and we may not eat well every day or have enough sleep. Stress that it is important not to feel overwhelmed about trying to do everything perfectly, all the time. Some pupils may put too much pressure on themselves and try to create the 'perfect person'. Perhaps the teacher could volunteer to share an area where he/she can improve and offer a personal goal. Ask pupils to consider two areas where they might improve and ask them to describe how they might go about improving that area.

• Reinforce the importance of relaxation and leisure activities and ask pupils to consider their favourite to draw on the back of the page.

Answers

1.–3. Answers will vary

Additional activities

• Pupils can work in pairs or small groups to create a survey which asks questions about a well-balanced lifestyle. Have pupils survey other classes, friends or family members. Pupils can write a summary about the results.

• Ask pupils to create a poem that shows how to balance your lifestyle or the importance of a well-balanced lifestyle.

Background information

To be the best person you can be, you need to have a healthy body and a healthy mind. There are many aspects to creating a healthy, balanced lifestyle:

• *physical – a healthy diet, rest, relaxation, leisure, exercise*

• *emotional/social – a positive self-esteem, understanding, coping and sharing different feelings, dealing with pressure and stress, creating good relationships, tolerating others, understanding differences, maintaining friendships*

Curriculum links

England	PSHE	KS 2	Know what makes a healthy lifestyle, and set personal goals.
Northern Ireland	PD	KS 2	Understand the benefits of a healthy lifestyle, including rest and set goals for improvement.
Republic of Ireland	SPHE	5th Class	Recognise and examine behaviour that is conducive and harmful to health; e.g. balancing work and relaxation and identify realistic personal goals.
Scotland	Health/PSD	Level C	Show their knowledge and understanding of what they do to keep healthy; e.g. leisure activities and set realistic personal goals.
Wales	PSE	KS 2	Take more responsibility for keeping their body safe and set targets for improvement.

To achieve a healthy lifestyle, it is important to balance a wide variety of factors. Some of these are:

- healthy food.
- lots of exercise.
- a good night's sleep.
- enough leisure time.
- good relationships.
- a positive, healthy mind.

1 Complete the profile to show how well-balanced your lifestyle is.

I always include these healthy foods in my regular diet.

These are the types of exercise in which I'm regularly involved.

During the week, I always try to get _____ hours sleep a night.

My sleeping habits are good/bad because

During my leisure time, I'm involved in

I have great relationships with these people:

I make sure I'm mentally healthy by

2 Choose two of the factors above that you may be able to work on to create a more balanced life. Describe how you can improve these areas.

_____

_____

_____

3 On the back of this page, draw your favourite relaxation activity.

Objective

- Understands that puberty is a time of change and that various factors can affect development for individuals.

The lesson

Discussion points:

- What is puberty?
- Do boys and girls go through the same stages, at the same times?
- What physical and emotional changes will happen?
- Why is it such a difficult time for some people?
- Why do we need to go through puberty?

What to do:

- Pupils need to understand that puberty affects boys and girls at different ages and even then, not all girls or boys go through the same things at the same times. It is important to be sensitive to individual pupils' experiences and to ensure no-one is singled out. Creating a warm, caring and honest environment will help to alleviate any embarrassment or pressure, so the pupils can feel comfortable in sharing their thoughts.
- Before beginning any class discussion, ask pupils to write, in their own words, what they think puberty is. Create a class list of pupils' ideas and discuss as appropriate.
- Ask pupils to decide if the statements presented are true or false and discuss answers.
- Discuss that there are different factors which will affect how individuals will develop through puberty. One of the most important influences involves heredity factors. Individuals who choose to lead a healthy lifestyle tend to develop within the 'average' range. Those who have poor diets and rarely exercise may develop at slower rates than their peers. Give examples of the factors mentioned and ask pupils to explain these in Question 3.
- Prior to a class discussion on the statement in Question 4, ask pupils to consider their feelings and write their opinion. Have pupils pair up with a member of the opposite sex. Ask pupils to take it in turns to explain their opinions, giving reasons. Pupils can then complete the second part of Question 4.
- Ask pupils to think about how it can sometimes be hard to feel different from everyone else. Reiterate the factors which influence development during puberty. Allow pupils time for discussion and to write a response to the situation given in Question 5.
- In advance of perhaps setting up a question and answer box/session, ask pupils to write three questions they would like to have answered in relation to puberty and the changes they may be experiencing.

Answers

1. Answers will vary
2. (a) false (b) true (c) true (d) false (e) false
3-6. Answers will vary

Additional activities

- Use some of the questions the pupils have written for Question 6 to create an advice column. After a class discussion, turn the questions over to another box and allow pupils to choose one. Have them read it and write their own advice or answers to the question posed. These could be included in a class newsletter or posted on a class web site.

> **Background information**
>
> *Puberty is the period of time during which a child develops to sexual maturity. Puberty is triggered by the release of hormones, which are released from the ovaries in girls and the testicles in boys. The female's eggs (ova) mature and the male produces sperm. Puberty begins around 10 – 14 years in girls and one or two years later in boys. The age at which puberty occurs depends on a wide range of factors, including heredity, diet, exercise and the amount of body fat. Puberty not only causes physical changes; the way young people think and act will also change.*

Curriculum links

England	PSHE	KS 2	Know about how the body and emotions change as they approach puberty.
Northern Ireland	PD	KS 2	Be aware of the physical and emotional changes that take place during puberty.
Republic of Ireland	SPHE	5th Class	Identify and discuss the physical and other changes that occur in boys and girls with the onset of puberty and understand that these changes take place at different rates for everyone.
Scotland	Health	Level C	Identify the different ways in which people grow and change; e.g. puberty.
Wales	PSE	KS 2	Understand the physical and emotional changes that take place at puberty.

1 In your own words, what is puberty?

_____

_____

_____

_____

_____

2 (a) Everyone starts puberty at the same age.

| true | false |

(b) Girls usually mature earlier than boys.

| true | false |

(c) Puberty is a time of change.

| true | false |

(d) The end of puberty is 15 years of age.

| true | false |

(e) Physical changes are exactly the same for everyone.

| true | false |

3 There are different factors that can have an influence on development through puberty. Give examples to explain the following factors:

(a) heredity

(b) diet

(c) exercise

4

'Girls have more things to deal with during puberty than boys.'

(a) Give your opinion on this statement.

_____

_____

_____

_____

_____

(b) Find a classmate of the opposite sex and write his/her opinion.

_____

_____

_____

_____

_____

_____

5 Wanita has been teased because she hasn't yet started to develop physically. Many of her friends are already wearing bras. What advice can you give Wanita?

_____

_____

_____

6 On the back of this page, write three questions you would like to ask someone you trust about puberty.

Objective

- Describes ways of coping with changes that occur during puberty.

The lesson

Discussion points:

- What are the physical and emotional changes that happen?
- What are some strategies for dealing with changes?
- Why is puberty a difficult period for some and not others?
- What are all the positive things about puberty and growing up?

What to do:

- Pupils need to understand that puberty affects boys and girls at different ages and even then, not all girls or boys go through the same things at the same times. It is important to be sensitive to individual pupils' experiences and to ensure no-one is singled out. Creating a warm, caring and honest environment will help to alleviate any embarrassment or pressure, so the pupils can feel comfortable in sharing their thoughts.

- Prior to a class discussion, ask pupils to list what they already know about the physical changes that occur to boys and to girls during puberty for Question 1. Ask pupils to volunteer their ideas to create a class list. Discuss issues, questions or experiences as they arise.

- Discuss different strategies for coping with changes that occur during puberty. Ask pupils to work in pairs or small groups to discuss the issues presented in Question 2 and offer strategies to cope. Pupils may wish to volunteer personal experiences or ideas to a class discussion.

- Ask pupils to consider the open-ended statements in Question 3 and write their responses for each.

Answers

1.–3. Answers will vary

Background information

Puberty starts when your brain sends messages to your body to start releasing hormones. Hormones are chemical substances that are produced in groups of cells called glands. Different hormones act on different parts of your body. Two of these hormones, oestrogen in girls and testosterone in boys, guide children to grow into adults. Hormones cause physical changes and emotional changes. It is perfectly normal to feel moody, sometimes for no reason at all. No two people are the same during puberty and everyone changes at his/her own pace.

Additional activities

- Pupils can work in small groups to create a pamphlet or poster that shows the best ways of coping with changes that occur during puberty.
- Have pupils role-play situations where they have to deal with some of the changes that will affect them during puberty.

Curriculum links

England	PSHE	KS 2	Know about how the body and emotions change as they approach puberty.
Northern Ireland	PD	KS 2	Be aware of the physical and emotional changes that take place during puberty.
Republic of Ireland	SPHE	5th Class	Identify and discuss the physical and other changes that occur in boys and girls with the onset of puberty and understand that these changes take place at different rates for everyone.
Scotland	Health	Level C	Identify the different ways in which people grow and change; e.g. puberty.
Wales	PSE	KS 2	Understand the physical and emotional changes that take place at puberty.

1 Write what you know about the physical changes that occur during puberty.

Girls	Boys

2 Describe some strategies to show how you might deal with the following issues.

Every morning I worry about how I look. I feel a bit chubby and some of my friends are skinny and tall.	*I have a party on Saturday and my face is covered in pimples.*
Every time my parents ask me to do something, I get so mad with them. I just want to go to my room and not talk to anyone.	*Sometimes I feel in a bad mood and sometimes I feel just great. It's a bit like a roller-coaster ride where you go up and down all the time. I hate feeling so moody.*

3 Complete the following.

(a) The best things about puberty and growing up are ...

(b) The things I find hardest to cope with are ...

(c) I think I'll be able to cope with all the changes because ...

Objective

- Describes aspects of social and emotional growth and development.

The lesson

Discussion points:

- What emotional changes might you experience during puberty?
- How and why can relationships change?
- Will everyone experience the same changes, at the same times?
- What are the best ways to deal with emotional changes?

What to do:

- Discuss how hormones released during puberty can dramatically alter moods, emotions and social behaviour. Provide examples of different issues and experiences to initiate a class discussion. Perhaps responses could be grouped under headings such as 'family' and 'friends'. Ask pupils to describe some of the changes they have experienced in relationships with parents, friends and siblings.

- The teacher may wish to use the issues in Question 2 as role-plays, where pupils work in pairs or small groups to act out the situations. Ask pupils to describe how they would deal with the situations.

- Ask pupils to consider the statements presented in Question 3 and decide whether they agree or disagree with them.

- Reflecting on class and group discussions, ask pupils to make a list of all the words they can think of which describe how they feel about the emotional changes of puberty.

Answers

1.–4. Answers will vary

> **Background information**
>
> During puberty, pupils will start to change the way they think. They start to choose their own standards and form their own ideas and values. Instead of relying on being part of a family, individual identity develops. Pupils are looking for more independence. The first point of conflict is often with family, as pupils try to assert their independence while still trying to retain some support. Peer pressure also becomes a major influence as pupils feel strongly about wanting to be more like their friends.

Additional activities

- Ask pupils to create a 'Did you know?' sheet that describes some of the emotional and social changes that can occur during puberty.
- Create a comic strip that deals with an emotional issue pupils may be faced with during puberty.

Curriculum links

England	PSHE	KS 2	Recognise, as they approach puberty, how people's emotions change at that time and how to deal with their feelings towards themselves, their family and others in a positive way.
Northern Ireland	PD	KS 2	Be aware of the emotional changes that take place during puberty.
Republic of Ireland	SPHE	5th Class	Identify and discuss the changes that occur with the onset of puberty and appreciate the need for individual space and privacy as he/she is growing and developing.
Scotland	Health	Level C/D	Identify the different ways in which people grow and change; e.g. puberty and demonstrate an understanding of their emotional needs.
Wales	PSE	KS 2	Understand the emotional changes that take place at puberty.

Puberty is the time when there are many physical changes happening to your body. There are also a lot of emotional changes that occur at this stage of your life. The quick release of hormones into your body can signal extremes in emotions and mood. This is only temporary. Dealing with all the physical changes can have an effect on your emotions, self-esteem and the way you relate to other people.

1 Describe any changes in the relationships you have with your:

(a) *parents* _____

(b) *friends* _____

(c) *siblings* _____

2 Everyone deals with conflicts and issues in different ways. Explain how you might deal with these situations.

You want your own space but your little sister keeps hanging around.	Your friends can always do things but your parents won't let you do the same.	Whenever you want privacy, your parents are always in your room.

3 Indicate whether you agree or disagree with these statements.

(a) I'm starting to form my own values and opinions about different things.

▮ **disagree**   **agree** ▮

(b) I know how to stick to what I believe is right.

▮ **disagree**   **agree** ▮

(c) I'm able to deal with the strong feelings and changes of mood.

▮ **disagree**   **agree** ▮

(d) I can take responsibility for my actions.

▮ **disagree**   **agree** ▮

(e) I have become a lot closer to my friends.

▮ **disagree**   **agree** ▮

(f) Peer group pressure has a positive influence on me.

▮ **disagree**   **agree** ▮

(g) I feel like I am becoming more independent.

▮ **disagree**   **agree** ▮

(h) I am in conflict more often with my family.

▮ **disagree**   **agree** ▮

4 Create a list of words which describe how you feel about the social and emotional changes of puberty.

Objective

• Recognises that changes occur in a consistent pattern although individuals are all unique.

Background information

There are various stages of puberty. Those shown are guidelines and not inclusive of all physical changes that will occur. It is essential that the tables presented are discussed so that pupils know that although everyone may follow the same pattern, not everyone will experience the changes at the same time.

The lesson

Discussion points:

• What are the different stages of puberty?
• Does everyone go through the same stage at the same time?
• Does everyone go through the same stages?
• When are you an adult?
• Why are some people bigger or smaller than others in the class?
• When would you expect a period to start?

What to do:

• Discuss the tables presented on the worksheet showing stages of puberty for boys and girls. Reinforce that the ages shown are average ages only and changes may occur outside these ranges. Pupils need to realise that the ranges are quite wide because individuals develop at different times, with different factors influencing these changes. Allow pupils opportunities to ask questions and discuss the tables as a class or in small groups. Pupils can highlight the changes that occur to both boys and girls.
• Complete Question 3 by answering true or false for each statement.

Answers

1.   Every person is unique and will develop at a different time.
2.   Hormones, height increase, change in body shape, pubic hair, underarm hair, skin may get more oily.
3.   (a) true (b) true (c) true (d) false (e) false (f) true

Additional activities

• Pupils could write a brief magazine article that describes different stages of puberty for boys and/or girls.
• Ask pupils to write a private diary entry that describes the stage of development they may be at and includes what their feelings may be.

Curriculum links

England	PSHE	KS 2	Know about how the body changes as they approach puberty.
Northern Ireland	PD	KS 2	Be aware of the physical changes that take place during puberty.
Republic of Ireland	SPHE	5th Class	Identify and discuss the physical changes that occur in boys and girls with the onset of puberty and understand that these changes take place at different rates for everyone.
Scotland	Health	Level C	Identify the different ways in which people grow and change; e.g. puberty.
Wales	PSE	KS 2	Understand the physical changes that take place at puberty.

During puberty, you will experience many changes. These changes follow a consistent pattern. Although the pattern for all of us is the same, we are also unique individuals.

Stages of Puberty for Girls

Stage	Age range (average)	Development
1	8 – 11	No obvious signs. Ovaries are enlarging and hormones are being produced.
2	8 – 14	The beginning of breast growth. Height and weight can increase. Fine and straight pubic hair is noticed.
3	9 – 15	Breast growth continues. Pubic hair becomes coarser and darker. Menstruation may start.
4	10 – 16	Underarm hair appears. Menstruation begins. Ovulation begins but may not be in a regular monthly cycle. Skin may get more oily.
5	12 – 19	Breast and pubic hair growth are complete. Menstruation is well established, with ovulation occurring monthly. Full height is attained.

Stages of Puberty for Boys

Stage	Age range (average)	Development
1	9 – 12	No obvious signs. Hormones are becoming active. Testicles are maturing. May start rapid growth late in this stage.
2	9 – 15	Testicles and scrotum begin to enlarge. Little increase in penis size. Some growth of pubic hair. Increase in height and change in body shape.
3	11 – 16	Penis starts to grow in length, not so much in width. Pubic hair starts to get darker and coarser. Height growth continues. Body/face looks more adult. Voice begins to deepen.
4	11 – 17	Penis width and length increases. Underarm hair develops. First ejaculations start. Facial hair increases. Voice gets deeper. Skin may get more oily.
5	14 – 19	Close to full adult height and physique. Facial hair grows and shaving may begin. Pubic hair and genitals have adult appearance. During late teens, chest hair may appear.

1 Why do you think the average age ranges are so wide?

_____

_____

2 Highlight those changes that happen in both girls and boys.

3 (a) Boys and girls will follow the same pattern of development. | true | false |

(b) Both boys and girls will change their body shape. | true | false |

(c) Girls generally mature earlier than boys. | true | false |

(d) All girls will start their period between 9 and 15. | true | false |

(e) All boys will develop at the same time. | true | false |

(f) A person's body is usually adult by the end of their teens. | true | false |

Objective

- Identifies the effects of various substances on the body.

The lesson

Discussion points:

- What are drugs?
- What drugs are available in our community?
- Why do people use drugs?
- Why are some drugs illegal?
- How do some drugs affect your behaviour?
- What are the negative effects of drugs?
- Are there any positive effects of drugs?
- What types of legal drugs have you used?
- Why do you think alcohol and cigarettes are legally available?

What to do:

- Ask pupils to contribute to a class list of drugs that they know. Highlight those that are legally available. Read and discuss the 'Did you know' facts presented on the worksheet. Pupils may wish to highlight facts.
- Have pupils work in small groups to discuss the positive and negative effects that the listed drugs can have on people. Are there more negative or positive effects?
- Why do young people use drugs, both legal and illegal? After discussion, ask pupils to rank the list showing why they think young people may use drugs, with number 1 being the most common reason.

Answers

See Background information for suggestions.

> **Background information**
>
> *Drugs, both legal and illegal, can affect a person in many different ways. These effects include injury/accidents, risk of infectious diseases, damage to body organs, depression, psychosis, stress, relationship problems, violence, legal issues, financial problems or antisocial behaviour. There are few positive effects. Prescribed medications have obvious benefits, if taken correctly. Caffeine may be used as a short-term stimulant.*

Additional activities

- Use the Internet to research the effects of a particular drug; for example, alcohol or tobacco.
- Create a poster that shows the effects of different drugs to discourage use.

Curriculum links

England	PSHE	KS 2	Know which commonly available substances are legal and illegal, their effects and risks.
Northern Ireland	PD	KS 2	Know about the harmful effects to themselves and others of tobacco, alcohol, solvents and other illicit and illegal substances.
Republic of Ireland	SPHE	5th Class	Distinguish between legal and illegal substances, examine and understand the effects they have and explore the reasons why people use them.
Scotland	Health	Level C	Show their knowledge and understanding of the impact of harmful substances on the body.
Wales	PSE	KS 2	Know about the harmful effects, both to themselves and others, of tobacco, alcohol, solvents and other legal and illegal substances.

Did you know?

A drug is any chemical that affects your body. Drugs can be medicines like pain-killers and antibiotics. They can also be substances that affect your mind rather than your body.

The most commonly used drugs in our society are alcohol, tobacco and prescription drugs. Marijuana is the most commonly-used illegal drug.

ZYBON

Keep out of reach of children.

Cigarette smoke contains around 4000 chemicals. Nicotine is the poisonous chemical that causes addiction.

—SKY—

CIGARETTES

All drugs, illegal and legal, can fit into one of three categories.

Stimulant (upper) — Speeds up the brain and nervous system. Caffeine, nicotine, amphetamines, cocaine and ecstasy are all stimulants.

Depressant (downer) — Slows down the brain and nervous system. Alcohol, marijuana, heroin, glue, analgesics and sleeping pills are all depressants.

Hallucinogens (psychedelic) — Alters a person's consciousness. LSD, ecstasy, magic mushrooms and marijuana are all hallucinogens.

1 Make a list of the positive and negative effects of the following legal drugs.

Drug	Positive effects	Negative effects
alcohol		
tobacco		
caffeine		
pain-killers		

2 Rank the following to show why you think young people may use drugs (1 should be the most common reason).

☐	stress	☐	for fun
☐	to experiment	☐	to celebrate
☐	to be one of the group	☐	to relax
☐	to forget about problems	☐	to feel more confident
☐	to relieve boredom	☐	to feel older

Objective

- Recognises that although cigarettes and alcohol are legal drugs, there are health and social risks associated with their use.

The lesson

Discussion points:

- Why do you think people may take up smoking?
- Why do you think some people still smoke even when they know it's dangerous to their health?
- Why and how does the government try to get people to quit smoking?
- How can you say no if you don't want to try smoking cigarettes?
- How does it make you feel when someone is smoking near you?
- Why is alcohol seen as a more socially acceptable drug in our society?
- What can happen when you drink too much alcohol?
- Why do people drink alcohol?
- What problems can be caused by misusing alcohol?

What to do:

- In small groups, or as a class, discuss reasons why young people may use alcohol and cigarettes. Ask pupils to list the main reasons for Question 1.
- Discuss the short- and long-term effects of alcohol and tobacco use. Ask pupils to decide which effects are short-term and which are long-term by marking the correct column in Question 2.
- Have pupils consider the benefits of choosing a lifestyle that does not include smoking cigarettes. Discuss as a class or in small groups. Pupils can choose the four most important reasons why they would benefit from a smoke-free lifestyle in Question 3.
- Ask pupils to discuss the statement in Question 4 in pairs and decide on their own opinions. Ask them to justify these opinions.
- Ask pupils what the average cost of a pack of cigarettes might be. Give them a figure to work with and have them calculate costs for a week, month and year. After they have found the totals, have them consider all the different things they could spend that money on if they were not buying cigarettes.

Answers

1. Answers will vary
2. Alcohol effects – short, long, long, short, short, long, short, long/short, long/short, short, short, long
   Cigarette effects – long, short, short, long, long, short/long, short/long, long, short/long, short, short/long, short/long
3.–5. Answers will vary

Background information

Research shows that smoking is the single greatest preventable cause of disease in the developed world. Smoking is a major cause of heart disease and contributes to many cancers, including lung, mouth, throat, stomach, kidney, pancreas, bladder and colon. Emphysema, ulcers, asthma and bronchitis are also linked to smoking.

There are approximately 4000 chemicals found in cigarette smoke, with about 40 identified as cancer-causing agents.

Passive smoking is the inhalation of other people's cigarette smoke.

Alcohol is a toxic drug that can poison the body. It is a depressant which slows down the brain and nervous system. It can damage all the major organs of the body. Although a legal drug, alcohol misuse can cause health, social and community-related problems. Alcohol affects all people differently. It can take about one hour for an average healthy adult to eliminate one standard drink of alcohol.

Additional activities

- Devise a survey to find people's opinions on a community-related issue in regard to smoking and alcohol; for example, 'smoking should be banned in all public places' or 'the legal age for alcohol should be raised to 21'.
- Use the Internet to research statistics about alcohol consumption and cigarette use. Compare countries around the world. Present findings to the class and display.

Curriculum links

England	PSHE	KS 2	Know which commonly available substances are legal and illegal, their effects and risks.
Northern Ireland	PD	KS 2	Know about the harmful effects, to themselves and others, of tobacco and alcohol.
Republic of Ireland	SPHE	5th Class	Understand the effects that legal substances have and explore the reasons why people smoke and drink alcohol.
Scotland	Health	Level C	Show their knowledge and understanding of the impact of harmful substances on the body.
Wales	PSE	KS 2	Know about the harmful effects, both to themselves and others, of tobacco and alcohol.

Alcohol and tobacco

1 Write some reasons why you think people may use alcohol and tobacco.

Reasons for alcohol use	Reasons for tobacco use

2 Shown below are some of the short-term and long-term effects of smoking cigarettes and drinking alcohol. Decide which are short-term and which are long-term.

Alcohol

Effect	Short	Long
loss of coordination	☐	☐
skin problems	☐	☐
heart disease	☐	☐
vomiting	☐	☐
aggression	☐	☐
liver damage	☐	☐
flushing and dizziness	☐	☐
loss of memory	☐	☐
depression	☐	☐
unconsciousness	☐	☐
loss of inhibitions	☐	☐
brain damage	☐	☐

Cigarettes

Effect	Short	Long
lung cancer	☐	☐
bad breath	☐	☐
smelly hair	☐	☐
emphysema	☐	☐
heart disease	☐	☐
stained teeth and fingers	☐	☐
high blood pressure	☐	☐
throat cancer	☐	☐
stomach ulcer	☐	☐
lack of oxygen to lungs	☐	☐
dry skin	☐	☐
lack of taste and smell	☐	☐

3 List four benefits of choosing a smoke-free lifestyle.

(a) _____

(b) _____

(c) _____

(d) _____

4 'Cigarettes and alcohol should be illegal drugs.'

Explain your opinion of this statement.

_____

_____

_____

5 Find out the cost of one packet of cigarettes. How much would one packet a day cost over ...

(a) one week? _____ (b) one month? _____ (c) one year? _____

(d) What could you spend this money on instead of cigarettes? _____

Objective

- Predicts and reflects in role-play situations on decisions to refuse cigarettes and alcohol.

The lesson

Discussion points:

- What is peer pressure?
- How can you say no to offers of cigarettes and alcohol?
- When is it important to stand up for yourself and make decisions?
- How did the characters in these role-plays justify their decisions?
- How well did the characters deal with the situations they were involved in?

What to do:

- The role-play cards on the following page should be cut out and given to pairs of pupils. The pupils must role-play the situation and decide on reasons to justify their actions. Teachers may like the pupils to choose a situation and perform it for the class or may like the pupils to try out each role-play over several weeks, perhaps performing them for another pair.
- Discussion should follow the performances of the role-plays. This can include looking at reasons for the situation and how the characters came to a decision.
- Encourage the pupils to use clear speech and gestures to show how the characters are feeling.

Answers

Teacher check

Background information

Peer pressure, parental values and self-esteem can often have an impact on how pupils cope with making decisions. Pupils need to be aware of the reasons why they may make certain decisions and how best to deal with potentially difficult decisions.

Additional activities

- Ask pupils to work together to devise their own role-play scenarios.
- Design posters to support positive decision making in various situations; for example, a poster could offer pupils suggestions for how to say no to drinking at a friend's house.

Curriculum links

England	PSHE	KS 2	Know that pressure to behave in an unacceptable or risky way can come from a variety of sources, including people they know, and be able to use basic techniques for resisting pressure to do wrong.
Northern Ireland	PD	KS 2	Develop strategies to resist unwanted peer and sibling pressure.
Republic of Ireland	SPHE	5th Class	Explore the role of personal choice and the influence of others when choosing to use non-prescribed substances.
Scotland	Health	Level D	Recognise that peer influence can affect choices they make.
Wales	PSE	KS 2	Recognise, understand and resist the power of unwanted peer influence and pressure.

A group of your friends are talking about trying alcohol at a party. Your religion doesn't allow you to drink alcohol. When you speak up, one of your friends starts to tease you.

How do you deal with this situation?

Your parents are having a discussion about a news report that says smoking should be banned in all public places. They are smokers and think it's a silly idea. You disagree.

How do you justify your opinion?

You look a little older than most of your friends. While out shopping, a friend dares you to go into a shop and buy a pack of cigarettes. You know it's not legal for the shop to sell them to you and you are worried about getting caught.

How can you tell your friend you won't take up the dare?

At your birthday party, you see a friend sneak some alcohol out of the fridge. You know this person has tried alcohol before. Your parents are very strict about alcohol and you're afraid they will catch your friend.

How do you approach your friend and what do you say?

The school football coach has warned the team that if he finds out anyone has been smoking, he will drop them from the side. A friend thinks that is a stupid rule and is sure the coach will not find out he has been smoking. He is the best player on the team.

How do you convince your friend not to take the risk of getting caught?

Your older sister is an asthmatic. She comes home one night and you know she has been smoking. You're worried about her health.

How do you tell her your concerns without her getting mad at you?

You are out with a group of friends. When a cigarette is passed around, you decide to try it just this once. Predict the consequences of your decision.

Every time you stay over at a friend's place, one of the adults in the house is always drunk. You don't feel comfortable staying there any more.

How do you speak to your friend about the situation?

While your older brother is having a party, you and a friend sneak some alcohol out of the fridge. No-one notices. During the night, your friend becomes really sick and starts to vomit.

Who do you approach?

At a family gathering, your dad passes you a small glass of wine to celebrate an important occasion. You hate the smell and don't want it.

How do you tell your dad that you won't take it?

Objective

- Recognises factors that influence participation in physical activities and the risks associated with a sedentary lifestyle.

The lesson

Discussion points:

- Why is keeping fit good for your health?
- What do you do to keep fit?
- How does physical activity help your body?
- How do you feel when you exercise?
- What are the dangers of not exercising enough?
- What benefits are there to your physical health?
- What are some different ways that you can stay fit and lead an active lifestyle?
- What are some of the obstacles to participating in physical activity? This may include medical conditions, culture, economics, availability of resources, personal choice or social problems.

What to do:

- Discuss the benefits of physical activity and the different groups into which activities can be categorised. Ask pupils to complete the table in Question 1 by adding more activities for each group.
- As a class, or in small groups, ask pupils to make a list of the different skills associated with physical activities on a separate sheet of paper. These may include balance, coordination, speed, agility, power or reaction time, as well as more specific bat and ball type skills. Have pupils draw a picture to represent a sport or activity that will improve the three skills stated in Question 2.
- Ask pupils to consider the health risks associated with a sedentary lifestyle. See Background information for factors to discuss. Allow pupils time to make a list of those health risks discussed to complete Question 3.
- To complete Question 4, discuss how different factors can have an influence on whether people participate in physical activity or not. Ask pupils to match the factors with the explanations given.
- Ask pupils to consider two goals they can set to improve their participation in physical activity. Discuss goal setting. Make goals simple, realistic and achievable.

Answers

1.   Stamina – aerobics, walking, jogging, cycling, dancing, etc.
      Strength – push-ups, weight-lifting, throwing, etc.
      Flexibility – gymnastics, cycling, etc.
2.–3.   Answers will vary
4.   Medical, Interest, Disability, Location, Cost, Time
5.   Answers will vary

Additional activities

- Write a magazine article describing the benefits of participating in physical activity. Use the Internet to find facts and pictures to support your article.
- Survey the class/year group to find the most popular physical activity in which pupils participate.

Curriculum links

England	PSHE	KS 2	Know what makes a healthy lifestyle, including the benefits of exercise and set personal goals.
Northern Ireland	PD	KS 2	Understand the benefits of a healthy lifestyle, including physical activity and set goals for improvement.
Republic of Ireland	SPHE	5th Class	Recognise and examine behaviour that is conducive to health and identify realistic personal goals.
Scotland	Health/PSD	Level C	Show their knowledge and understanding of what they do to keep healthy; e.g. regular exercise and set realistic personal goals.
Wales	PSE	KS 2	Understand the benefits of exercise and set targets for improvement.

Background information

To maintain a healthy lifestyle it is vital to include some form of physical activity in your day. Some experts recommend finding 30 minutes a day to devote to some sort of physical activity. Participating in physical activity has physical, social and emotional benefits. Physical activity can help with weight control, a healthier heart, improved lung capacity, clearer skin, good muscle tone, better sleep patterns and more energy. It can also provide teamwork skills, discipline, commitment, improved self-esteem and confidence.

1 Activities that improve physical fitness can be grouped into the following areas. Suggest different activities to complete the table.

Area	Benefit	Suitable Activities
Stamina	Improves the ability of muscles to work for longer periods, promoting endurance.	swimming,
Strength	Builds muscles.	rowing,
Flexibility	Allows for a wide range of movement of joints.	stretching,

2 Illustrate a sport or activity that will improve these skills.

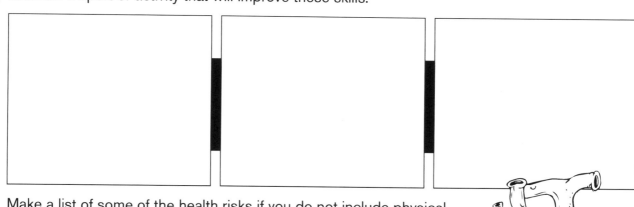

3 Make a list of some of the health risks if you do not include physical activity as part of your lifestyle.

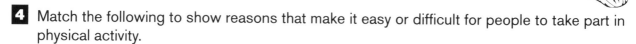

4 Match the following to show reasons that make it easy or difficult for people to take part in physical activity.

Cost •

Location •

Time •

Medical •

Disability •

Interest •

• My asthma condition prevents me from participating sometimes.

• I don't mind all the training because I love the sport.

• Being partly blind in one eye means I can't always hit the ball.

• The training venue is too far away for me to get to.

• The sport I love is too expensive to be involved in.

• I am already involved in music, drama and public speaking.

5 Write two goals that will help to improve your physical fitness.

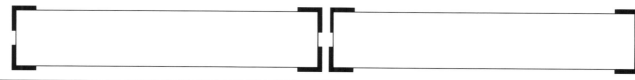

Objective

- Identifies aspects of the environment that may prove unsafe.

The lesson

Discussion points:

- What areas in your local environment make you feel unsafe?
- What situations make you feel unsafe?
- How can the local environment be improved to make it safer?
- What strategies can be put in place to make the environment safer?

What to do:

- Have pupils work in pairs or small groups to discuss the scenarios presented on the worksheet. Discuss how to recognise the problem in each. Ask pupils to consider a possible solution for each scenario.
- For Question 2, ask pupils to consider the different facilities in their local environment that help them to lead a healthy lifestyle. Make a class list of some of these facilities. Have the pupils choose one facility and describe how it contributes to a healthier lifestyle.

Answers

1. Possible solutions:
    - (a) Choose another route, walk home with a group, write to the council and ask for a patrol in the area.
    - (b) Contact the council, see if any adults can help to fix it.
    - (c) Install a fence, plant bushes, install lighting.
    - (d) Stay indoors, call the police, turn on the lights.
    - (e) Contact the council, ask adults to help you clean it up, put up signs, choose somewhere else.
    - (f) Turn and walk in the opposite direction, go to a shop, get the licence number.
2. Answers will vary

Background information
Many people have come to realise that one of our basic needs in life is a healthy environment. We can choose to become involved in making changes to our lifestyles so the things we do decrease the detrimental impact on the environment. We can also undertake activities to improve the environment.
For young people, getting involved with tree planting, cleaning up rubbish, recycling and fundraising for threatened species are just a few easy ways to learn how to care responsibly for the natural world.

Additional activities

- On a local map, label the facilities that help provide pupils with a healthier lifestyle.
- Ask pupils to write a formal letter to the local council, raising an environmental issue that affects them in some way.

Curriculum links

England	PSHE	KS 2	Recognise the different risks in different situations, decide how to behave responsibly and know where to get help and support.
Northern Ireland	PD	KS 2	Cope with their environment safely and know where, when and how to seek help.
Republic of Ireland	SPHE	5th Class	Identify situations and places that may threaten personal safety and develop strategies for keeping safe.
Scotland	Health	Level D	Identify strategies for keeping healthy and safe and ways in which the wider community takes action to protect health.
Wales	PSE	KS 2	Know what to do or whom to go when feeling unsafe and be concerned about the wider environment.

1 Identify the problem in the following scenarios and plan a solution for each.

(a) The shortest way home from school is through a park where there is a public toilet that often has older people hanging around.

Problem:

Solution:

(b) The closest basketball court is old and a lot of the surface is cracked and uneven. You have already tripped and hurt yourself before.

Problem:

Solution:

(c) The dark alley behind your house is used by many people and you worry that someone might break into your house.

Problem:

Solution:

(d) Your parents are due home shortly but you're sure a stranger is outside your house.

Problem:

Solution:

(e) The park that you and your friends go to is often littered with glass and you don't feel safe playing there.

Problem:

Solution:

(f) You are walking home from the shops and you think someone is following you in a car.

Problem:

Solution:

2 Draw a facility in your local environment that contributes to you leading a healthy lifestyle.

Name of facility:

This place helps to keep me healthy by

Objective
- Recognises emergency situations and how to deal with them.

The lesson

Discussion points:
- How do you know if a situation is an emergency?
- How do you deal with emergencies?
- When is it time to call emergency services?
- What basic first aid do you need to know?

What to do:
- Ask pupils to volunteer to relate any situations they have been involved in that would be classed as an emergency. What happened? What was the correct response? What was the outcome? Discuss basic first aid (see Background information). Pupils may work in pairs or individually to complete the table in Question 1 to show the correct responses to given emergency situations.
- Pupils can work in small groups to discuss an action plan for the given situations in Question 2. Pupils can research correct procedures on the Internet or use the library for further information.
- Discuss how accidents and emergency situations can affect anyone. Some situations may be more prevalent in particular age groups; for example, toddlers may swallow objects, small babies may stop breathing, the elderly may fall and break bones. Ask pupils to consider the different age groups and write two situations in which they think that group is more at risk.

Answers
1.   (a) house fire – get out of the house, call the fire brigade
     (b) swimmer – alert lifeguard/lifeboat service, watch for the swimmer
     (c) electric shock – turn off power, move the victim if safe, call ambulance
     (d) rider – call ambulance
     (e) overdose – call an ambulance
     (f) bee sting – administer drug, call ambulance

2.–3. Answers will vary

Additional activities
- Ask pupils to role-play the action plans that were devised in Question 2 and present them to the class.
- Create a poster that alerts others to emergency situations and details what to do and when to use emergency services.

Background information

Everyone needs to be able to identify when a situation is an emergency and what to do in the circumstances. Basic first aid courses can be accessed through the St John Ambulance Association. It is important for pupils to recognise the importance of using emergency services only when necessary. If they are able to recognise an emergency situation correctly, then they are less likely to make unnecessary use of the ambulance, police and fire services. For information on the accepted response in emergency situations visit:

www.sja.org.uk
www.redcross.org.uk
www.redcross.org.ie

Curriculum links

England	PSHE	KS 2	Know about basic emergency aid procedures and where to get help and support.
Northern Ireland	PD	KS 2	Be aware of basic emergency procedures and first aid and know where, when and how to seek help.
Republic of Ireland	SPHE	5th Class	Know what to do in the event of an accident; e.g. using simple first aid procedures and knowing how to use the emergency services.
Scotland	Health	Level C	Show safe ways of dealing with a range of situations, particularly those that may present risk.
Wales	PSE	KS 2	Know what to do or whom to go to when feeling unsafe and develop practical skills necessary for everyday life.

1 Describe the correct emergency response to the following situations.

Situation	Response
(a) A fire starts in the kitchen.	
(b) A swimmer is caught in a strong current.	
(c) A family member receives an electric shock.	
(d) A bicycle rider is hit by a car.	
(e) A young child swallows a handful of headache tablets.	
(f) Your older brother is allergic to bees and has just been stung.	

2 Work out an action plan to show how you would deal with the following emergencies.

Three friends are lost in the woods.

At a party, a young person overdoses on an unknown drug.

3 Write two emergency situations that the following groups of people may be affected by.

babies

teenagers

toddlers

adults

children aged 5 – 12

the elderly

Objective

- Recognises influences on safe behaviour and the use of safety equipment.

The lesson

Discussion points:

- What safety precautions do you take in different situations?
- How do you deal with unsafe situations?
- What safety equipment do you use for different activities?
- Why is it important to look at the consequences of your decisions?

What to do:

- Survey the class to see how many wear a helmet every time they ride their bikes. Talk about the use of safety equipment and why it is so important. Discuss different activities and the equipment needed for each. Ask pupils to write the safety equipment required in the situations to complete Question 1.

- Provide a situation where the pupils need to make a decision that could affect their safety and discuss as a class. Look at the options, consequences and then the response that might be made. Talk about the importance of making correct decisions regarding safety and risk-taking behaviour. Pupils can work in pairs to discuss the scenarios presented in Question 2 and consider the options, consequences and responses they would make.

- Discuss the factors that may have an influence on safety precautions taken; for example, with friends you might be sure to stay together, make sure someone knows where you are, have access to an adult to come and get you. Involvement in sport might see correct safety equipment used. Allow pupils time to discuss the safety precautions they may take to complete Question 3.

Answers

1.   (a) helmet (b) seatbelt (c) helmet (d) life jacket (e) knee/elbow pads, helmet (f) life jacket (g) safety harness, helmet (h) helmet
2.–3. Answers will vary

Additional activities

- Design a poster to encourage the wearing of bicycle helmets or other safety equipment.
- In pairs, have pupils propose their own situations that require them to consider options and consequences. These can be written on cards, with pupils role-playing the situations.

Background information

The vast majority of people who are hurt by others are usually hurt by those they know. Even though many people are not hurt by strangers, it is important to take sensible precautions and be prepared. Some ideas to reduce the chances of unsafe situations are:

- *Try to use transport rather than walking alone.*
- *Plan ahead and let an adult know where you are.*
- *Carry coins for a public phone or carry a mobile phone.*
- *Walk in groups and choose the streets that are most lit and busy.*

Curriculum links

England	PSHE	KS 2	Recognise the different risks in different situations, decide how to behave responsibly and know where to get help and support.
Northern Ireland	PD	KS 2	Develop a pro-active and responsible approach to safety and know where, when and how to seek help.
Republic of Ireland	SPHE	5th Class	Discuss a variety of risky situations and behaviour and assess and evaluate how these risks may be avoided or minimised and the implications of taking risks.
Scotland	Health	Level C	Demonstrate simple decision-making strategies in relation to keeping healthy and safe.
Wales	PSE	KS 2	Develop decision-making skills and know what to do or whom to go to when feeling unsafe.

Primary health and values Prim-Ed Publishing - www.prim-ed.com

1 What safety equipment do you need in the following situations?

(a) riding a bicycle

_____

(b) driving in a car

_____

(c) riding a motorcycle

_____

(d) sailing on a yacht

_____

(e) using rollerblades

_____

(f) waterskiing

_____

(g) abseiling

_____

(h) riding a horse

_____

2 Complete the table to show ways that you might respond to different situations by looking at the options and consequences.

Situation An adult is dropping you at a friend's house. You know the adult has been drinking alcohol. *Options* *Consequences* *Response*	*Situation* You are walking home alone and you know someone is following you. *Options* *Consequences* *Response*
Situation Your friends are jumping off a bridge into a river. You are not a strong swimmer. *Options* *Consequences* *Response*	*Situation* You have been in a chat room on the Internet with someone you thought was your age. You now think the person might be lying and he wants to meet with you. *Options* *Consequences* *Response*

3 What safety precautions do you take ...

(a) when you are with friends?

_____

(b) when you are alone?

_____

(c) when you are involved in sport?

_____

(d) when you are at home?

_____

Objective

- Recognises that there are different factors which influence our choice of health products and services.

The lesson

Discussion points:

- What influences the health products we choose?
- What is the difference between name brands and generic brands?
- Do different advertisements appeal to different groups of people?
- Where would you find information about health services and products?
- What health services do you use?

What to do:

- If possible, bring in two similar products which are different brands. Discuss prices and why people would choose each brand. What factors would influence their choice? Survey the class to see which they would choose. Ask pupils to give their own reasons to explain why people may buy a more expensive product in Question 1.
- Ask pupils to consider some of the different health products they use. Complete the table in Question 2 by writing in the brand name of each product and giving a reason for selection.
- Pupils will need access to a variety of magazines and newspapers. Have them select two advertisements that show a health product. It would be beneficial for the teacher to present an advertisement to the class first and discuss the table. Allow pupils time to complete the table for Question 3.
- Make a class list of the different factors that can influence the choices we make in buying different health products. Discuss examples of each factor presented. Ask pupils to list health products they would use for each of the factors shown in Question 4.
- Discuss the different health services that pupils might use in the local community. Ask them to make a list of the places where they would find information to access these services.

Answers

1.–5. Teacher check

Background information

There are often a variety of factors which have an influence on the types of health products and services we might choose. Some of these include price, location (of service), availability, time of year, illness, personal preference, advertising, self-image, culture, religion and safety.

Additional activities

- Use the Internet to find sites where information regarding health issues can be accessed.
- Create an advertisement for a health product or service that would appeal to your age group.

Curriculum links

England	PSHE	KS 2	Know how to make informed choices and explore how the media present information.
Northern Ireland	PD	KS 2	Explore and examine what influences their views and the role of advertising.
Republic of Ireland	SPHE	5th Class	Explore and examine critically the factors that influence choices and become aware of the purpose of advertising.
Scotland	Health	Level D	Recognise that peer and media influences can affect choices they make.
Wales	PSE	KS 2	Know about the role of advertising.

1 There are two sunscreen products available. One is a home brand in a plastic tube. The other is a name brand in a bottle, at double the price. Give reasons to explain why people might buy the more expensive sunscreen.

2 What brands of health products do you use? Explain why you choose each brand.

Product	Brand	Reason
toothpaste		
shampoo		
deodorant		
sunscreen		
soap		
headache pill		

3 Find two advertisements in a magazine or newspaper that show a health product. Complete the tables.

Product

Who would the advertisement appeal to?

Why would someone choose the product?

Would you buy it?

Product

Who would the advertisement appeal to?

Why would someone choose the product?

Would you buy it?

4 There are often many different factors that can influence the choices we make to buy certain health products.
List health products you may be influenced to buy because of each factor.

family _____

friends _____

cost _____

advertising _____

personal preference _____

5 Make a list of some of the places you would look to find information about health products and services.

Objective

- Recognises that different factors influence decisions regarding food selection.

The lesson

Discussion points:

- What are some of the factors that have an influence on food selection?
- What is your 'perfect meal'?
- Would your parents have different influences from you?
- What cultural factors influence food selection?
- Do you like to try new foods?
- Are you a fussy eater or will you eat anything?

What to do:

- As a class, or in small groups, make a list of the different factors that can influence the types of foods we choose to eat. Ask pupils to draw and label food choices that are influenced by the factors listed in Question 1.
- From the class or group list, ask pupils to write any other factors which affect their food choices.
- Ask pupils to complete Question 3 by answering yes or no to each statement.
- Discuss how different groups of people may be influenced by different factors when making food choices. Highlight different age groups and situations such as babies, adults, the elderly and situations like Christmas, birthdays and Easter. Ask pupils to consider the influences that may affect their parents when making choices about food. These may include money, availability, culture, family preferences, medical conditions and ease of preparation.
- Have pupils describe their perfect meal and then consider the factors which have influenced this choice.

Answers

1.–5. Answers will vary

Background information

It is important to make wise decisions about what you eat. A range of factors can influence what you choose. The following categories include influences that may affect a pupil's eating habits.

- *family – economics, location, cooking skills, parental preferences*
- *media – appealing advertising, interest in trying something new, 'specials' advertised*
- *cultural – family staple foods, family recipes, religion, special occasions*
- *health/medical – special diets for illness/medical conditions/ weight/allergies*
- *seasonal – availability of foods, different foods during winter/ summer months*

Additional activities

- Use the Internet or library resources to research different foods available around the world.
- Create a survey to find out what influences pupils' parents to make the food choices they do.

Curriculum links

England	PSHE	KS 2	Know how to make informed choices and explore how the media present information.
Northern Ireland	PD	KS 2	Explore and examine what influences their views and the role of advertising.
Republic of Ireland	SPHE	5th Class	Explore the factors that influence food choices.
Scotland	Health	Level D	Recognise that peer and media influences can affect choices they make.
Wales	PSE	KS 2	Recognise and understand the power of peer influence and pressure and know about the role of advertising.

1 Draw and label foods you might be influenced to select for the following reasons.

availability	peers	advertising
family	**culture**	**personal preference**

2 List any other factors that might influence your food selection; for example, medical influences, location.

3

Advertising has a big influence on the foods I like to eat.	yes	no
My parents make most of the decisions about what foods I eat.	yes	no
I usually go grocery shopping with my parents.	yes	no
I like trying foods from other cultures.	yes	no
Health has a lot to do with the foods I choose to eat.	yes	no
I'm influenced by my friends when choosing snacks to eat.	yes	no
I tend to be a very fussy eater.	yes	no
I prefer home-cooked meals to takeaway meals.	yes	no
I think adolescents are more influenced by the media than adults.	yes	no
I'll eat just about any food put in front of me.	yes	no
Image has a lot to do with the food choices I make.	yes	no

4 What factors do you think influence the food choices your parents make?

5 Describe your 'perfect meal'. Make a list of the different factors that have influenced this choice.

Objective

- Understands that media images may not always promote a realistic representation.

The lesson

Discussion points:

- Who is your favourite media personality?
- How is body image depicted in the media? Is it realistic?
- Why do we look the way we do?
- What makes a 'perfect' person?
- What does it take to make models look so good?

What to do:

- Discuss different media personalities. Who appeals most? Why? Are all the favourites younger personalities? Are there any older role models? What qualities do you think these personalities have?
- Provide the pupils with examples of advertisements that show models, both young and more mature. Pupils could work in small groups and look through the advertisements. Have them decide if the body image presented in each is realistic and achievable. Do younger or older models provide a more realistic image? Pupils can respond to the statement presented in Question 2 and give an example to support their views.
- Ask pupils to find an advertisement that shows clothing, make-up or a grooming product. Ask them to describe the models used. Are they young, slim, healthy, beautiful? Do these models represent the age group the advertisement is targeted at? Is this realistic? How would someone be influenced to buy the product? How effective is the advertisement?
- Allow pupils time to answer yes or no to the statements presented in Question 4.
- Provide pupils with a variety of magazines. Ask them to look through the magazines and cut out body parts they think are 'ideal'. Have them glue them together to make a 'perfect' person. Reinforce that no-one is perfect and be sure to have a good laugh at the creations!

Answers

1.–5. Answers will vary

> ### Background information
>
> *Many advertisements which target adolescents use models that may not represent a realistic body image. With some pupils experiencing low self-esteem and a poor body image, it is important they understand that advertising campaigns can be unrealistic.*

Additional activities

- Create a mural that shows different advertisements representing positive and negative body images.
- Write a poem on body image and how to feel good about the body you have.
- Write a letter to a friend, telling them all their good points and why you like being his/her friend.

Curriculum links

England	PSHE	KS 2	Feel positive about themselves and explore how the media present information.
Northern Ireland	PD	KS 2	Examine the role of advertising and how the media present information and develop their self-esteem.
Republic of Ireland	SPHE	5th Class	Accept his/her own body image and explore factors that affect his/her self-image; e.g. advertising.
Scotland	Health	Level D	Recognise the link between body image, self-worth and external influences.
Wales	PSE	KS 2	Have respect for their body and know about the role of advertising.

Why do you look the way you do? Mostly, it's genetics. You have genes from both parents, so you look like members of your family. How you look also depends on how you look after yourself. Often, people in the media are portrayed as 'perfect'. They have plenty of help to look the way they do in public. Many models in advertisements present an 'ideal' person but it is often unrealistic and unachievable. Did you know there are body doubles for feet and hands? Airbrushing, special lighting and computers are also used to make models look perfect.

1 (a) Which media personality do you admire the most?

_____

(b) Make a list of the qualities you think this personality has.

[ ]

'The body images presented in the media are positive ones.'

2 Explain your opinion of this statement. Provide an example to support your views.

_____
_____
_____

3 Find an advertisement for clothing, make-up or a grooming product. Glue on the back of this page.

(a) Write words to describe the model used.

[ ]

(b) Is the model an 'average' representation of his/her age group? Why/Why not?

_____
_____
_____

(c) Why do you think someone would choose the product?

_____
_____
_____

(d) Is the advertisement effective or ineffective? Why/Why not?

_____
_____
_____

4 I think most advertisements are realistic.

yes   no

I often think I would like to look like one of the models in a magazine.

yes   no

I have a positive image of myself and my body.

yes   no

Advertisements influence my decisions to buy different products.

yes   no

5 Use magazines to make a collage of a 'perfect' person. Cut out body parts from famous people you think are ideal. Glue them together and have a good laugh!

Objective

- Recognises positive and negative influences of peers on behaviour.

The lesson

Discussion points:

- Why are friends so important?
- What kind of positive and negative influences can your peer group have?
- What type of group member are you?
- How do you deal with peer group pressure?

What to do:

- As a class, or in small groups, have pupils discuss why friends are important to them. If working in small groups, it may help to break already established friendship groups and form groups that may not be so close. Ask pupils to consider the major reasons why their friends are important to them and record these to complete Question 1.

- Encourage pupils to consider their roles within their peer group and tick those statements that are true for them to complete Question 2.

- As a class, discuss how the peer group can have a positive or negative influence on all of us. If possible, teachers could relate personal experiences of negative and positive situations; for example, the peer group encouraged you to reach a certain goal, the peer group talked you into taking a risk that you knew wasn't safe. Ask pupils to consider the positive and negative influences the peer group can have on the behaviour listed in Question 3.

- Pupils can work in pairs to discuss the two situations presented in Question 4 before making up their own minds about what they would do in each instance.

Answers

1.–4. Answers will vary

> **Background information**
>
> *The peer group can have negative and positive influences on individuals.*
>
> *Positive influences can include opportunities for rewarding friendships to develop, to share dreams, emotions and leisure activities, to develop social skills and to develop self-awareness.*
>
> *Negative influences can include exerting pressure to behave in ways that are against the individual's beliefs, suppressing the individual and encouraging members to conform to certain ideals and behaviour.*

Additional activities

- Create an acrostic poem that highlights both positive and negative influences of the peer group. The poem could be titled 'Peer Influences'.
- Create a comic strip that shows a situation where the peer group is having a negative or positive influence on the individual.

Curriculum links

England	PSHE	KS 2	Know that pressure to behave in an unacceptable or risky way can come from a variety of sources and use basic techniques for resisting pressure.
Northern Ireland	PD	KS 2	Develop strategies to resist unwanted peer pressure and behaviour.
Republic of Ireland	SPHE	5th Class	Explore how the opinions, views or expectations of others can influence how people relate to each other, either positively or negatively.
Scotland	Health	Level D	Recognise that peer influences can affect choices they make.
Wales	PSE	KS 2	Recognise and understand the power of peer influence and pressure.

1 My friends are important to me because …

2 Within my peer group, I …

am a leader. ☐

am a decision maker. ☐

am easily influenced by others. ☐

prefer to listen to others. ☐

have strong views on what we should do. ☐

always stand up for myself. ☐

feel pressure to do what everyone else wants to. ☐

am a risk taker. ☐

3 Consider how your peer group can have a positive and negative influence on the following behaviours.

Behaviour	Positive	Negative
personal exercise		
diet		
taking risks		
use of drugs		
self-esteem		
purchases you make		
goals you set yourself		

4 (a) You have saved some money to put a deposit on a guitar you want. Your parents are going to pay for the lessons and music is a major interest in your life. Your group of friends are all going to a theme park and want you to come with them. You don't want to blow all your deposit money but you don't want to be 'left out' either. What decision do you make?

(b) You have decided you need to do more exercise so you can get fit. You write up a plan to exercise three days a week after school. You usually spend this time with your friends, doing homework together or just hanging out. How do you explain the importance of sticking to your goals?

Objective

- Makes judgments on the reliability of advertisements.

The lesson

Discussion points:

- What forms of information do we normally think of as 'the media'?
- What type of advertisements do you like?
- What makes a good or bad advertisement?
- Why has cigarette advertising been banned in many countries?
- What information should be included on product labels?
- How is alcohol presented in the media?

What to do:

- If possible, show some previously-taped television advertisements and have magazine and newspaper advertisements displayed. Survey pupils to find their favourite and least favourite advertisements. Are the class favourites directed at adolescents? What are the common products advertised? Are role models involved? Allow pupils time to write their favourite and least favourite in the given media categories in the table in Question 1.
- What factors make an advertisement popular? Make a class or group list of factors that make advertisements good or bad. What annoys you about advertisements? Ask pupils to list those factors that they think make a great or terrible advertisement to complete Question 2.
- Discuss how cigarette advertising has been banned in many countries for some time. Ask pupils to give reasons why. Read out some of the warnings displayed on cigarette packets and discuss their impact. Do they make a difference to smokers? Non-smokers? Ask pupils to give their responses to complete Question 3.
- Ask pupils to consider different advertisements for alcohol products on television and in magazines. If possible, have some examples for pupils to look at. Discuss the images presented in the advertisements. Who do these advertisements appeal to? Who are the advertisements targeted at? Ask pupils to complete their responses in Question 4.
- If possible, provide some product labels for pupils to look at. Ask them to consider the different information presented on each. Who reads the labels? Does the information presented on a label influence your choice? What other information could be included? Pupils can complete Question 5 by considering what information may be most important to them.
- Ask pupils to create their own labels that include all the information they think should be included.

Answers

1.–6. Teacher check

Additional activities

- Write a letter to an editor of your favourite magazine, giving your opinion of the way products for adolescents are advertised in their publication.
- Make a collage of magazine advertisements that you consider present realistic information.

Curriculum links

England	PSHE	KS 2	Explore how the media present information.
Northern Ireland	PD	KS 2	Explore the role of advertising.
Republic of Ireland	SPHE	5th Class	Explore some of the reasons why people smoke or drink alcohol; e.g. influence of advertising.
Scotland	Health	Level D	Recognise that media influences can affect choices they make.
Wales	PSE	KS 2	Know about the role of advertising.

Background information

Advertising in the media—television, radio, magazines, newspapers and the Internet—can often have a huge impact on the decisions we make about what to spend our money on. Advertisers use different approaches and images to entice people to buy their products and use their services. The media can present information, products and services that may be relevant to our lifestyle. Many health products and services are widely advertised through the media.

1 What is your favourite and least favourite advertisement in the following media categories?

	Favourite	Least favourite
(a) television		
(b) radio		
(c) Internet		
(d) magazines		

2 (a) What makes a great advertisement?   (b) What makes a terrible advertisement?

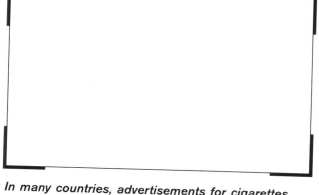

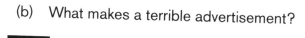

In many countries, advertisements for cigarettes are banned in the media and for sponsorship of sport. Cigarette packets show government health warnings such as 'Smoking Kills' and 'Smoking Causes Cancer'.

3 (a) Why do you think cigarette advertising is banned in many countries?

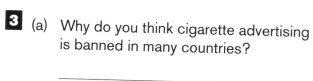

(b) Do you think the information presented on cigarette packets will help people to quit? Give a reason for your answer.

4 Consider advertisements in magazines and on television for alcohol products.

(a) What types of images do these advertisements usually promote?

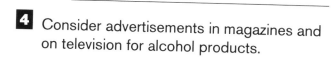

5 When you look at a label on a product you are about to purchase, what information do you take notice of?

(b) What age group is usually targeted in these advertisements?

6 Think of a product you might buy regularly. On the back of this page, create a label that shows all the information you think should be included for that product.

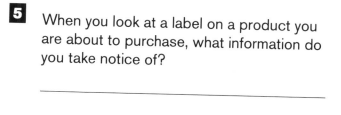

Objective

- Describes actions required to address a specific personal health issue.

The lesson

Discussion points:

- What personal health issue concerns you the most?
- What makes up an action plan?
- What do you need to achieve set goals?
- Why are goals important?

What to do:

- Ask pupils to consider personal health issues that are important to them. Have them choose one issue for which they can develop an action plan. Provide an example to use and work through the plan with the whole class. Allow pupils time to reflect on a goal and complete the action plan. Decide on an achievable time frame to reach goals. This activity could be presented as a home completion assignment.

Answers

Teacher check

Background information

A healthy body and mind make it easier to cope with any challenges or difficult times that face us. It is important to make exercise, eating properly and getting enough sleep priorities at any age. By creating an action plan, goals can be reached and success achieved.

Here are some suggestions for personal health goals:
- *be more active,*
- *sleep more,*
- *eat less junk food,*
- *eat more fruit and vegetables,*
- *make time to relax,*
- *be less stressed,*
- *spend less time worrying about what I look like and more time thinking about what I feel like, and*
- *improve my personal hygiene.*

Additional activities

- Pupils can work in small groups to develop a plan to solve a school or community health issue.
- Pupils can write an article that describes how they solved a personal, family, school or community health issue.

Curriculum links

England	PSHE	KS 2	Set personal goals.
Northern Ireland	PD	KS 2	Set goals for improvement.
Republic of Ireland	SPHE	5th Class	Identify realistic personal goals and targets and the strategies required to reach these.
Scotland	PSD		Show ability to set realistic goals.
Wales	PSE	KS 2	Set targets for improvement.

My Action Plan

My personal health issue is:

These are the concerns I have:

My goal is to:

These are the steps I plan to take:

This is what I need to achieve my goal:

This is how long it will take to reach my goal:

This is who can help me:

This is where I can find out more information to support my plan:

Now I've achieved my goal, here is my reflection on the plan:

Objectives

- Identifies ways in which people stay fit.
- Recognises factors that influence people's choices of participation in activities to stay fit.

The lesson

Discussion points:

- Why is it important to become or stay physically fit?
- Do you have to play a sport to keep physically fit? How else can you stay fit?
- How do you stay physically fit?
- How do members of your family stay fit?
- Why do you think people choose different ways to stay fit?
- Do adults and children choose the same ways to stay fit?

What to do:

- Ask pupils the meaning of the word 'pastime'. (Something enjoyable to do that passes the time.) Discuss how pastimes can be physical or non-physical.
- Ask pupils to suggest other non-physical pastimes than those listed.
- The first three discussion points above should enable pupils to answer Question 1. Pupils can work in pairs to complete the activity.
- Discuss findings as a whole class. List the reasons why pupils chose the physical activities on the blackboard/whiteboard.
- Pupils complete Question 2 independently.
- The table in Question 3 will need to be completed at home, or information gathered from an adult and brought to school to complete. Pupils could ask a parent, relative, neighbour or adult family friend.
- Discuss the findings in the table, noting similarities and differences between it and the table from Question 1, before completing Question 4.

Answers

1.–4. Teacher check

Additional activities

- Review both tables to see similarities and differences between males' and females' choices of physical activity.
- Complete the table after interviewing someone in the 16 – 20-year-old age bracket. Compare results.

Background information

There are numerous physical activities people can participate in to stay fit. Physical activity must be undertaken regularly to maintain or improve fitness. Team sports are popular with a variety of age groups. Individual sports, such as swimming, judo, tennis or golf can be engaged in by joining a club or special class, or participating in at leisure. Other activities such as walking, jogging, rollerblading, skateboarding, bike riding or kicking a football around can be done with a friend, group of friends or individually.

Several factors influence people's choice of sport or physical activity. Many pupils around the age of 10 to 12 will be involved in team sports through physical education classes at school, playing for their school or being a member of a club outside school. Sports may include netball, football, cricket, rugby or hockey. Pupils will also participate in pursuits such as bike riding, walking to and from school (or the bus stop!) and skateboarding.

Many adults still participate in vigorous sports or activities. Some prefer golf, Tai Chi, walking, yoga and lawn bowls to contact sports.

Besides age, other factors influencing choice of physical activity include family, peers, school and coaches, culture, media and advertising, geographic location, and what the individual enjoys.

Curriculum links

England	PSHE	KS 2	Know what makes a healthy lifestyle, including the benefits of exercise.
Northern Ireland	PD	KS 2	Understand the benefits of a healthy lifestyle, including physical activity.
Republic of Ireland	SPHE	5th Class	Recognise behaviour that is conducive to health; e.g. taking adequate exercise.
Scotland	Health	Level C/D	Show knowledge of physical needs and what they need to do to keep healthy; e.g. regular exercise.
Wales	PSE	KS 2	Understand the benefits of exercise.

How do people keep fit?

Physical activities strengthen our heart and lungs, develop our muscles and improve our range of movement.

1 List physical activities you do, or could do, to keep physically fit. Sort them into team sports or individual sports and activities. For those in which you actually participate, write where you do them and why you do them.

	Where	Why
Team sport		
Individual sport or activity		

2 After a discussion with your class, list the three main reasons you think pupils choose to do physical activities.

(a) _____ (b) _____ (c) _____

_____ _____ _____

3 Ask an adult about the physical activities in which he/she participates and complete the table below.

	Where	Why
Team sport		
Individual sport or activity		

4 Explain the similarities and differences between the two tables.

similarities _____   *differences* _____

_____   _____

_____   _____

Primary health and values

Objective

- Recognises personal feelings related to given statements.

The lesson

Discussion points:

- How well do you know yourself?
- Do you think you have good self-esteem?
- How do you think you would react in an emergency?
- Do you like talking about yourself?

What to do:

- Use the worksheet as a one-to-one conference, a portfolio activity or as a teacher record.

Answers

Answers will vary

Background information

Body language such as facial expressions, stance and posture are keys to knowing how a person is feeling. Different situations evoke different emotions. Pupils should be aware that each of us may react to different situations in different ways. Other situations may evoke a similar emotion such as excitement towards a birthday party. Pupils need to learn to show feelings in ways that are helpful to them and others, and not in ways that are hurtful.

Additional activities

- Pupils complete a 'report card' about themselves, giving themselves a score out of 10 on areas such as attitude, decision making, effort, confidence and other similar attributes.
- Pupils complete the report card with a personal comment of how they can improve their scores in the above areas. They write themselves an achievable goal.

Curriculum links

England	PSHE	KS 2	Deal with their feelings.
Northern Ireland	PD	KS 2	Examine and explore their feelings and emotions.
Republic of Ireland	SPHE	5th Class	Identify and discuss a range of feelings.
Scotland	PSD		Recognise a range of emotions and have views on their aptitudes.
Wales	PSE	KS 2	Be still, reflect and know the range of their feelings.

My thoughts and feelings

Answer yes or no.	Yes	No
1. I eat a well-balanced diet.		
2. I like setting myself goals and achieving them.		
3. I get on well with my peers.		
4. I always wear a bicycle helmet when I'm riding.		
5. I like new challenges.		
6. I enjoy being physically active.		
7. I prefer quieter, less active activities.		
8. I could improve my diet.		
9. I get plenty of sleep.		
10. I find it easy to make friends.		
11. I am confident in speaking my opinions.		
12. I am a good team member.		
13. I feel shy when speaking out.		
14. I find it hard to get to sleep.		
15. I do not mind being alone sometimes.		
16. I like my appearance.		
17. I should do more exercise.		
18. I have lots of interests.		
19. I wish I looked different.		
20. My friends influence what I do.		
21. I know how to respond to unsafe situations.		
22. I am a positive person.		
23. I am able to find enough time to relax.		
24. I'm comfortable with the changes of puberty.		
25. I always take responsibility for my actions.		
26. I experience some conflict with my family.		
27. I'm confident of resisting any pressure to use drugs.		
28. I am able to set goals to improve my lifestyle.		
29. I use community facilities to keep fit.		
30. I'm confident I can recognise an emergency situation and deal with it.		
31. I cope well with peer pressure.		
32. I'm able to select foods that are good for me when I make my own choices.		
33. I enjoy including a variety of different foods in my diet.		
34. I understand that the media may not always promote things realistically.		
35. I'm able to make decisions with confidence.		
36. I have a positive body image.		
37. Close relationships are important to me.		
38. My parents influence a lot of what I am able to do.		
39. I'm an emotional type of person.		
40. I enjoy getting up each morning.		

Objectives

- Understands the terms 'role' and 'responsibilities'.
- Identifies own roles and responsibilities within different groups.
- Comments on how he/she carries out each role and suggests personal improvements.

The lesson

Discussion points:

- What is a 'role'?
- What is meant by 'responsibility'?
- Discuss roles and responsibilities of different age groups – toddlers, school aged children, teenagers, adults.
- At what age do responsibilities begin? End? (If at all!)
- Do people respond to responsibilities the same way?
- Do roles and responsibilities change with age? Environment? Circumstances?
- Do you enjoy all of your roles?
- How responsible are you?

What to do:

- Ask pupils what they think the terms 'role' and 'responsibility' mean. List responses on the blackboard/whiteboard. Pupils can use these to refer to when answering Question 1.
- Read and discuss the paragraph about personal roles with the whole class. Ask several pupils to define their roles so all pupils will gain a clear understanding of what is required in Question 2. Remind them to think of what they do at home, at school, in clubs and teams or in the community.
- Pupils will probably provide more honest responses to Questions 2 – 5 if working independently. Discuss what is involved in each question, then assist as required.
- Those pupils who wish to could share responses with the class.

Answers

1.–5. Teacher check

Additional activities

- In small groups, rehearse then role-play certain roles, showing irresponsible and responsible behaviours for each. Discuss what each performance is trying to show.
- As a class, devise a checklist of how to be a responsible person.
- Use characters in novels to discuss their roles and how responsible or irresponsible they were.

Background information

A person's 'role' is the expected or usual part played in life. People have different roles; for example, a teacher has a professional role at school and roles at home as possibly a wife/husband/partner or parent. A responsibility is a duty of care. Within each role, a person has certain responsibilities to perform. Roles and responsibilities change with age and environment.

Roles and responsibilities help to shape a person's character. It is important children are given responsibilities for this reason. These will:

- provide them with chances to show their knowledge, skills and understanding of what is required.

- develop their self-worth, provide a reason for doing something and encourage commitment to keep going.

People do not all respond in the same way to responsibilities. Shy, less confident people may not enjoy or even take on leadership roles in a group, but may work well within a group and still be responsible.

Others may act irresponsibly and cannot be relied upon. Some people are more responsible in some roles than others.

Curriculum links

England	PSHE	KS 2	Know there are different kinds of responsibilities and duties at home, school and in the community.
Northern Ireland	PD	KS 2	Identify a variety of groups and their roles and responsibilities.
Republic of Ireland	SPHE	5th Class	Identify different groups to which they can belong and recognise the roles of individuals.
Scotland	PSD		Adopt different roles within groups and reflect on and evaluate their roles.
Wales	PSE	KS 2	Maintain relationships and take increasing responsibility for their actions.

What do you think the words 'role' and 'responsibility' mean?

1 Use keywords and phrases to explain each word.

Role	Responsibility

People have more than one role, especially as they get older. Your roles might include being a pupil in your class, a member of a club or team, a son or daughter and a brother or sister. Your roles are at school, home and in the community. You have certain responsibilities within each role.

2 Choose up to six of your roles and explain your responsibilities for each. Give yourself a mark out of 10 for how well you carry out each role. (10 being the best.)

Role	Responsibility	Rating

3 Now consider how responsible you are overall. Rate yourself (10 being the most responsible).

1	2	3	4	5	6	7	8	9	10

4 (a) What role are you best at?

_____

(b) Why do you think this is?

_____

_____

_____

_____

5 Could you improve the way you behave in certain roles?

yes   no

Explain.

_____

_____

_____

_____

Objectives

- Participates in teamwork activities requiring cooperation and communication.
- Identifies the qualities of good teamwork.
- Evaluates teamwork performance of his/her group.

The lesson

Discussion points:

- How did your group cooperate?
- What problems did your group encounter? How were they solved?
- What are good groupwork qualities?
- What are good leadership qualities?
- Were you happy with your group's performance? Why/Why not?

What to do:

- Divide the class into groups of five or six. Pupils will be given an activity to complete and evaluate. The groups who work well collaboratively will be more successful.
- Explain to the pupils that talking to group members is vital to complete the activity successfully. The whole group must agree on each decision before it is carried out.
- Explain the following activity to the pupils.

  Objects and shapes
  - Each of the following objects or shapes is to be made in their group.
  - Every group member should be part of the object or shape.
  - Each person must hold his/her pose for at least 10 seconds.

- Choose from the following (or use your own). You must use at least four.
  - a pentagon or hexagon
  - an irregular shape (hold up a diagram or draw on the board).
  - a camel   – a monster   – a settee   – an elephant
  - a can-opener   – a peg   – a whisk   – a car
  - a bicycle   – a television

- Pupils should complete the activity without viewing the other teams.
- When the activity is completed, each group can present a selection of the shapes or objects to the class.
- Read through Question 1 with the whole class. Discuss the list of considerations before pupils complete the question individually. Responses can be shared and discussed within their groups.
- Question 2 can be completed within these groups. Common keywords and phrases can be listed on the blackboard/whiteboard.
- Questions 3 to 5 should be completed individually after being read through and the meaning of unfamiliar words discussed. Leadership qualities can be listed as above.

Answers

1.–5. Teacher check

Additional activities

- Repeat the activity using a different group combination.
- Write dictionary definitions for words used in Questions 2 and 3.
- List teams/groups each pupil is involved in.

Curriculum links

England	PSHE	KS 2	Participate and develop relationships through work.
Northern Ireland	PD	KS 2	Maintain positive relationships and reflect upon their progress.
Republic of Ireland	SPHE	5th Class	Practise ways of working together.
Scotland	PSD		Carry out tasks in a group.
Wales	PSE	KS 2	Work cooperatively to tackle problems.

Background information

The qualities of an effective team include:

Working towards a clear goal – the team clearly understands and works towards the goal that is to be achieved. Team members are focused on the tasks they are allocated by the team. The team defines any targets that need to be achieved as it works towards the common goal.

Good communication – the team members listen to each other with respect and willingly share their ideas without domination. Through this, the team members develop a mutual trust. Logical decisions are made with the acceptance of all team members.

Consideration – the team members encourage and support each other's ideas, giving critical feedback. Any criticism is aimed at the idea, rather than the person who contributed the idea. This encourages a willingness for the team to take risks and create new ideas. Everyone has an important role in the team.

The activities on the worksheet foster team skills such as communication, cooperation, negotiation, working towards a goal, problem-solving, allocating tasks, performing leadership roles, risk taking and creative thinking. They will also reinforce the concept that team members depend on each other for the whole team to work well.

1 Now you have completed the shapes and objects activity, finish the evaluation below to see how you and your team went.

Consider the following questions when commenting.

- Did the team have a clear understanding of the task?
- How was this done?
  Were problems discussed and dealt with?
- Did team members listen to each other?

- Did everyone participate?
- Did someone become a leader?
  If so, how did they perform this role?
- Did everyone agree with the decisions?

Team evaluation

Team members:

_____

_____

_____

Task:

_____

_____

_____

Comment on and rate how well the task was completed by your team (10 being the best).

1	2	3	4	5	6	7	8	9	10

_____

_____

You will have noticed that each team did not work in quite the same way. Some of the teams would have worked cooperatively, some would have worked in a disorganised way and some may have had a team member take on the role of a leader.

2 From what you have learnt from this activity, list keywords and phrases to describe the qualities of a good team.

3 Circle the qualities below you think would describe a good leader. Add more of your own.

disorganised	kind	bossy
a good listener	in control	helpful
gives suggestions	organised	polite
includes everyone	confident	rude
well-spoken	focused	loud
assertive	passive	timid
understanding		

4 How do you think you perform as a member of a team?

_____

_____

5 How do you think you perform as a team leader?

_____

_____

Objective

- Completes an identity map about himself/herself.

The lesson

Discussion points:

- What is your position in your family?
- What roles or responsibilities do you have at home?
- What characteristics do you share with other members of your family?
- What adjectives would you use to describe yourself to another person?
- What are your best and worst qualities?
- What qualities do you look for in a friend?
- How did you choose your best friends?
- What things helped to make you the person that you are?
- How do you think the media influences the behaviour of viewers?

What to do:

- Discuss the questions above. Read the opening paragraph with the pupils and discuss any unknown words or phrases. Read Question 1 to the pupils and be sure to allow pupils time to ask questions if they are unsure of what to do. Make sure that pupils write roles and responsibilities in this section.
- After completing Question 1, read Question 2 with the pupils, making sure they use adjectives to describe themselves. Pupils should then complete Question 3. Allow pupils to share their answers if they wish. Teachers may collect the completed worksheets for perusal, but no answer should be considered right or wrong, since it is a pupil's personal opinion. Teachers may gain an insight into how individual pupils see themselves.

Answers

1.–3. Answers will vary

Additional activities

- Create a family tree showing at least two generations.
- Make a Venn diagram or graph showing common characteristics such as birth dates, hair and eye colour, common interests and same number of family members.
- Create the 'ideal' pupil/friend/brother by selecting the most desirable characteristics and listing them on a chart.
- Pupils may work in groups to create the 'ideal' person and label with the most desirable qualities.

Background information

It may be difficult for pupils to have a clear view of themselves. They exist in a community which expects them to play different roles, many of which involve different behaviours. They are constantly being bombarded with media expectations of body images and materialistic values. They are moulded by their own experiences, by culture, sexuality and socio-economic status and peer, familial and gender influences. It is important for pupils to be aware that each of them is a multifaceted, unique individual who is valuable.

Identity grows as pupils relate to different people in different places.

Feelings and thoughts are more difficult for pupils to express, but play a valuable part in defining who a person really is and how they respond to others.

Curriculum links

England	PSHE	KS 2	Recognise their worth as individuals and realise that similarities and differences between people arise from a number of factors.
Northern Ireland	PD	KS 2	Develop self-awareness and understand that similarities and differences between people arise from a number of factors.
Republic of Ireland	SPHE	5th Class	Recognise and appreciate that each person is a unique individual.
Scotland	PSD		Know themselves as unique individuals.
Wales	PSE	KS 2	Recognise the uniqueness of individuals and feel positive about themselves.

No two people are the same. We look, think and behave differently. Each of us is unique and special.

Our identity is defined by our family, our friends, our cultural background, our hobbies and interests, our likes and dislikes, our experiences and our values and beliefs.

1 Use the map below to represent aspects of your identity. You should include roles or responsibilities that you have such as brother, nephew, grandson, friend, goalkeeper, pupil, school prefect etc.

2 Repeat the activity, but this time include character traits, such as loyal, funny, friendly, short-tempered, creative etc.

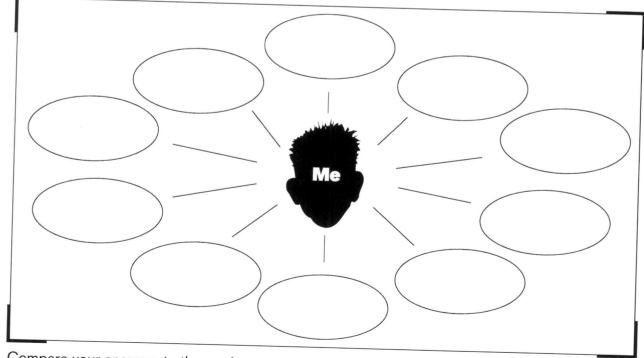

3 Compare your answers to those of someone else. Draw a cross on any traits which are similar and circle any traits which are different.

Objectives

- Selects strategies to develop self-esteem.
- Writes positive statements or words about himself/herself.
- Compares descriptions about himself/herself.

The lesson

Discussion points:

- Why do we need to feel good about ourselves?
- What does a confident person look like?
- What things give offence to yourself or others?
- Why shouldn't we criticise others?
- Why is it good to say how we feel?
- Why isn't it good to dwell on bad things that happened in the past?

What to do:

- Discuss the questions above. Read the list of things which encourage low self-esteem and discuss them. Pupils complete Questions 2 and 3. A friend should complete the first box in Question 4, then return the worksheet to the owner for him/her to complete the second box. The pupil then compares the two lists.

Answers

1. Answers will vary
2. Answers will vary, but may include the following:
   - (a) Make a decision and stick to it. If it is the wrong one, so what? We all make mistakes, but we learn from them.
   - (b) Ignore other people when they say something bad. No-one is perfect! Tell yourself some good things about yourself.
   - (c) Try not to say many bad things about yourself or others. 'If you can't say something nice, then say nothing!'
   - (d) Say how you feel if someone upsets you. This will develop communication and relieve tension.
   - (e) Forget what has happened before. You can't change the past! Each day can be a new beginning. Be positive and start afresh.
3.–4. Answers will vary

Additional activities

- Role-play standing tall and walking confidently.
- Encourage 'assertive' behaviour rather than aggressive behaviour.
- Practise saying 'I' statements to express feelings and what you would like to happen.
- Practise saying positive things about someone or something.
- Compile a list or chart for each pupil using positive words or sentences. Read it each day.

Background information

Self-esteem can be encouraged in the classroom through drama games, praise and encouraging empathy among pupils. Pupils can talk to each other in a positive manner, have positive friends, set small goals and aim to reach them, show positive body language (such as standing up straight without arms folded in front) and help others.

It is important that the pupils are aware of the need to:

- *Say positive things to themselves.*
- *Think positive things about themselves.*
- *Learn to accept that someone may look better than them, is thinner or has nicer hair today. Their only concern is themselves and no-one else. Developing self-esteem is a long-term process. Always aim to encourage and give praise when it is due.*

Curriculum links

England	PSHE	KS 2	Recognise their worth as individuals by identifying positive things about themselves.
Northern Ireland	PD	KS 2	Develop their self-esteem.
Republic of Ireland	SPHE	5th Class	Identify and learn about healthy ways to help him/her feel positive about himself/herself.
Scotland	PSD		Be positive about themselves and understand the importance of valuing self.
Wales	PSE	KS 2	Feel positive about themselves.

Self-esteem deals with how we feel about ourselves. If you feel confident and good about yourself, we say you have high self-esteem. If you feel bad about yourself and have no confidence, we say you have low self-esteem.

1 Read this list of habits which encourage low self-esteem.

(a) *Doubt yourself constantly.*

(b) *Take offence easily.*

(c) *Criticise yourself and others.*

(d) *Keep your feelings to yourself.*

(e) *Keep thinking about the bad things that have happened to you.*

2 Write a strategy to counteract each of the habits from Question 1.

(a)

(b)

(d)

(c)

(e)

3 Complete the statements below using positive thoughts.

(a) '*I am important because* _____

_____

_____

_____ '

(b) '*I am a good friend because* _____

_____

_____

_____ '

4 Ask a friend to write positive words about you in the first box, then complete the second yourself. Compare them when you have finished.

My friend's list	*My list*

Objectives

- Understands the meaning of the term 'stereotype'.
- Identifies and describes stereotypes in real life and on television.
- Realises the way people are treated according to a stereotype can affect their self-concept.

The lesson

Discussion points:

- When you meet someone for the first time, what is the first thing you notice about him/her? Is this the same for people in all age groups you meet?
- What makes you decide you like some people more than others?
- List qualities of your best friends.
- Do you know what someone is really like by appearance alone?
- What is a stereotype?
- Do you wish to be like certain stereotypes? If so, which ones?
- What kind of a person are you?

Materials needed/Preparation:

- Pictures of stereotypical male and female models from magazines and catalogues.

What to do:

- Distribute several of the pictures of stereotypical models to groups of pupils. Direct them to discuss in their groups what kind of people they represent and why they came to that conclusion.
- Discuss findings as a class. All or most groups should have decided the pictures were of models. List the reasons they came to that conclusion. Discuss other suggested answers, if any.
- Pupils can complete Question 1 individually.
- Read and discuss the information about a stereotype. Complete Question 2 individually or with a partner. Compare answers within the group. Were they mostly the same or different? Sex of character? Age of character?
- Discuss stereotypes on television. List suggestions given by the pupils. They can work in pairs to complete Question 3. Ensure they use a range of different programmes. Discuss how these stereotypes are treated.
- Relate the treatment of stereotypes to those in real life. Discuss how this can affect someone's self-concept.
- Read through the information relating to Question 4 with the pupils.
- Pupils complete the activity and compare answers.

Answers

1.–4. Teacher check

Additional activities

- Pupils can group themselves according to various categories such as gender; eye, skin or hair colour; birth date or month; food, sport or hobbies; likes and dislikes; height or weight (be sensitive about this one); and street name or number. This activity will help them realise how we can all fit into different 'stereotypes' or categories.
- Write a diary entry of a time you have been part of a stereotypical reaction—to yourself or someone else.

Background information

A stereotype can be described as a very simple— and often incorrect—picture that people have of a particular type of person. Stereotypes depend on conventional ideas about groups of people which may include attitudes, interests, characteristics, traits, mannerisms or physical appearance. It is common to base initial judgments about people on stereotypes.

Stereotyping can affect a person's self-concept, by others making unfair assumptions about his/ her skills, abilities and behaviour. Pupils need to learn to accept themselves so they can develop an open-minded attitude to others.

Many people compare themselves to others and try to fit into a stereotype. The media have a big influence on creating stereotypes. Television, in particular, uses symbols such as clothing, gestures, settings, physical appearance, behaviour and body language to create stereotypes that an audience can easily identify.

Curriculum links

England	PSHE	KS 2	Recognise and challenge stereotypes.
Northern Ireland	PD	KS 2	Explore and examine what influences their views and recognise how injustice and inequality affect people's lives.
Republic of Ireland	SPHE	5th Class	Explore how inequality might exist and suggest ways it might be addressed; e.g. stereotyping.
Scotland	Health	Level D	Recognise issues of discrimination.
Wales	PSE	KS 2	Respect others and recognise how injustice and inequality affect people's lives.

1 (a) What did your group decide about the
type of person the pictures represented? _____

(b) Explain how your group came to that conclusion. _____

_____

(c) Did all or most groups come to the same conclusion?   **yes**   **no**

Each group based its decision upon recognising a stereotype. A stereotype is a fixed idea people have of a particular person. The picture is easily recognised and understood by others who share the same view.

2 (a) Write descriptive words and phrases about what you think each of these people would look like.

A superhero	A rock star	A drunk

(b) Compare your answers with others in your group.

Many stereotypes can be found on television in commercials, soaps, films and comedy shows. Even news programmes select certain types of people to be newsreaders.

3 Complete the table below, using stereotypical characters from different television programmes or commercials.

Character's name and description	TV programme/commercial

You have seen the way in which stereotypes are treated on television; for example, popular characters in soaps have lots of friends. Unpopular characters do not. In real life, people can also be treated fairly or unfairly according to the stereotype they appear to be.

4 Read these scenarios and describe how each person might be feeling.

Bree is a very thin girl and quite short for her age. At lunchtimes, a popular game is for girls in her year group to choose teams to play netball. Bree is nearly always chosen last. Even then, she hardly gets much of a game and is often a 'reserve'.	*Ramil is new to his school. Being from an Indian background, he has dark hair and skin and brings different foods from home for lunch compared to the other pupils. He is finding it hard to make friends.*

Objective

- Identifies and categorises scenarios into those that are bullying and those that are not.

The lesson

Discussion points:

- Define bullying. Give examples of physical, verbal and social bullying.
- Discuss if 'one-off' situations are bullying or not.
- What makes someone want to bully?
- What are the consequences of bullying—to the person bullying and the person being bullied?
- How can bullying be stopped or prevented?

What to do:

- This activity can be completed in small groups. Have pupils suggest examples of physical, verbal and social bullying. Stress that bullying is deliberate and repeated over time.
- Pupils can answer Question 1 in their groups and report back to the class to compare answers.
- Discuss Questions 2 and 3 as a class before pupils answer individually.

Answers

1.–3. Teacher check

Additional activities

- Pupils can role-play bullying situations, then discuss what can be done to stop the situation happening again.
- Describe bullying situations seen during news bulletins, cartoons, soaps or drama programmes on television and discuss.

Background information

People who bully do so for many reasons. They may set out deliberately to bully and feel pleasure in bullying. It may give them a sense of power. People who bully may not necessarily lack self-esteem or be insecure. Many have average or above-average self-esteem. Their temperaments are more aggressive and they lack empathy. This can be caused by poor parenting and a lack of good role models or be a personality trait that needs fostering in a positive direction.

A summary of reasons includes:
- *They may feel upset or angry or feel they don't fit in.*
- *They want to seem tough and show off.*
- *They may get bullied themselves by family members.*
- *They're scared of getting picked on so they do it first.*
- *If they don't like themselves they may take it out on someone else.*
- *They think they will become more popular.*

Bullying can be divided into the following categories: physical, social/emotional, verbal, intimidation, written, discrimination and criminal.

Note: Criminal activity should be handled by the police or other appropriate authorities.

Curriculum links

England	PSHE	KS 2	Realise the nature and consequences of bullying.
Northern Ireland	PD	KS 2	Recognise, discuss and understand the nature of bullying and the harm that can result.
Republic of Ireland	SPHE	5th Class	Recognise, discuss and understand bullying and its effects.
Scotland	Health	Level C	Show safe ways of dealing with a range of situations; e.g. bullying.
Wales	PSE	KS 2	Understand the nature of bullying and the harm that can result.

Bullying is deliberately hurting other people with words or actions that are repeated over a period of time. Bullying can be physical, verbal or social. The person bullying has more power (physically or psychologically) than the person being bullied.

1 Decide if each of the situations below is a form of bullying. Explain why or why not.

1 Amber and Brittany are the only two girls in their class not invited to another's slumber party. The other girls are constantly talking about it in front of Amber and Brittany.

2 *Emill is a year older than the others in his class. He finds schoolwork difficult, especially reading. Being older, he is also noticeably more physically mature than the other boys. Several pupils constantly tease him and call him names such as 'you big dork' and 'moron'.*

3 Dylan and his friends wait at one of the entrances to the school on most days. Some younger pupils leave the school by another entrance to avoid being pushed, shoved or tripped up by the group.

4 During the holidays Georgia had her hair cut and restyled. Her mum also bought her a new pair of the latest shoes. Since then, some girls in her class have been whispering behind her back and laughing.

5 *Hannah and Kate scare younger pupils into giving them part of their lunch money. They threaten to pinch them and hurt them or to damage their school bags.*

6 *Harry is nearly always the last to be chosen on a team for a football match. Flynn told him it was because he was too fat and slow.*

Situation	Form of bullying? Probably/Probably not	Why or why not?
1		
2		
3		
4		
5		
6		

People who bully do so for a variety of reasons. They may or may not be aware of how their bullying makes others feel.

2 Add to this list of reasons why people bully.
(a) They see it as a way of being popular.
(b) They may be jealous of the people they are bullying.
(c) It makes them feel tough or important.
(d) _____
(e) _____
(f) _____

3 How might a person feel who is being bullied?
What effects could it have on him/her?
Write your thoughts on the back of this sheet.

Objective

- Considers the positive and negative effects peer pressure has on influencing behaviour and self-concept.

The lesson

Discussion points:

- What is meant by 'peer pressure' and 'peer influences'?
- Can peer influences be positive and negative? How?
- List personal positive and negative peer influence experiences.
- How can you say no to a situation you know is wrong?
- How does peer influence affect self-esteem?

What to do:

- Discuss the introductory paragraph with the pupils.
- Pupils can work in pairs to answer Questions 1 and 2 before sharing findings with the class. (Some pupils may not wish to share their answers to Question 2.)
- Discuss Questions 3 to 5 with the class and list keywords and phrases on the blackboard/whiteboard for them to refer to. Pupils can then answer those questions individually.

Answers

1.–5. Teacher check

Additional activities

- Role-play solutions to the negative scenarios on the activity page. Pupils can work in groups to prepare the role-plays to perform for the class.
- Discuss how a peer group can influence the following: your appearance, the music you listen to, what you buy with your money and your entertainment and leisure time.

Background information

Peer pressure is allowing others to influence your thoughts and actions. People who wish to 'belong' to a group are often swayed by peer pressure to follow the group's ideas and actions. Some experts believe that people who feel they belong to a group often feel more confident and their idea of self-worth increases. When in a group, people do not need to make decisions as the group tells them what to do and think.

It is important that people believe in their own self-worth and have confidence in their own thoughts, feelings and actions. People with confidence and who believe in themselves are often less likely to be swayed by negative peer pressure.

Peer pressure is not always a bad thing. People can influence others to improve their behaviour such as quitting a bad habit or improving their skills or sport. Some schools have used positive peer pressure to reduce the occurrence of bullying.

Curriculum links

England	PSHE	KS 2	Know that pressure to behave in an unacceptable or risky way can come from a variety of sources and use basic techniques for resisting pressure.
Northern Ireland	PD	KS 2	Develop strategies to resist unwanted peer pressure and behaviour.
Republic of Ireland	SPHE	5th Class	Explore how the opinions, views or expectations of others can influence how people relate to each other, either positively or negatively.
Scotland	Health	Level D	Recognise that peer influences can affect choices they make.
Wales	PSE	KS 2	Recognise and understand the power of peer influence and pressure.

We are all influenced by our peers (people our own age) to some degree. This is called 'peer pressure'. Our peers can influence both our thoughts and actions. We do something because 'the group' did it, instead of making the choice ourselves. Peer influences are not always negative – they can be positive too!

1 Decide if each of the situations below is an example of positive or negative peer influence. Explain why.

> **1** Corey's friends Matt, Ben and Aidan want him to jog around the local park every afternoon after school to practise for the interschool cross-country race.

> **2** Phoebe and Zoe have scratched the names of boys they like onto the bark of a tree in the park near the school. They want Emily to do the same.

> **3** Connor and Liam have told Declan he can only ride his BMX bike with them on the local bike track if he doesn't wear a helmet.

> **4** Shona, Mahlia and Taryn are taking tennis lessons on Wednesdays after school. They are trying to persuade Jade to join too, so they can play doubles together.

> **5** Mrs Townsend's class is arranged in groups of six. One group has started throwing bits of eraser and balls of paper at other groups when she is out of the class. They want the other groups to do the same.

Scenario	Positive/Negative	Reason
1		
2		
3		
4		
5		

2 Write a positive and negative example of peer influence you have experienced.

✓	✗

3 Why do you think people give in to peer pressure?

4 How can peer influences make you feel good about yourself?

5 On the back of this sheet, add to this list of advice about resisting negative peer influences.

- Feel good about yourself. It will help you to be strong enough to say no.
- Listen to yourself. It will help you to be strong enough to say no.
- Listen to your conscience about what is right and wrong.

Objectives

- Reviews current and past friendships.
- Evaluates himself/herself as a person in order to develop friendships.
- Establishes strategies to make new friendships while maintaining existing friendships.

The lesson

Discussion points:

- What type of friend are you?
- What qualities do you look for in a friend? Explain why.
- How can you make new friends?
- Why would you want to make new friends?
- Do you ever feel left out? Explain the situations or reasons for these feelings.
- How do friendships with members of the opposite sex change as you grow older?
- How do you cope with changes in your friendships?

Materials needed/Preparation:

- A4 sheets of plain paper
- organise pupils into groups of five or six

What to do:

- Begin by discussing the first question from the Discussion points. Offer pupils information about the skills involved in being a good friend from the Background information. Encourage pupils to describe themselves as a friend.
- Distribute sheets of paper and ask pupils to record keywords and phrases to describe their current friendships on one side. Are they happy and positive? Do they feel they are an equal or are they the leader? On the other side record the same information about past friendships. Have the pupils discuss the information recorded on the sheet with their peers in small groups.
- Direct pupils to Question 1 on the worksheet. This activity may require some real soul-searching for some pupils while others may find it easy. Read through the adjectives and explain any terms pupils may not understand before asking them to complete the activity.
- Discuss the second question from the Discussion points in small groups. Pupils then complete Question 2 on the worksheet. Encourage pupils to share some of their words and record these on the board. Discuss whether there were some common qualities all pupils looked for in a friend.
- Discuss the third and fourth questions from the Discussion points as a whole class. Pupils then complete Questions 3 and 4 on the worksheet.

Answers

1.–4. Answers will vary

Additional activities

- Work in pairs to role-play how they would begin to develop a new friendship.
- Write a newspaper advertisement looking for a new friend. Pupils will need to clearly and succinctly describe the qualities they are looking for in a friend.
- Discuss the fifth and sixth questions from the Discussion points in small groups and report main ideas to the whole class.
- Pupils discuss and draw a map to show how friendships change over time and include brief explanations of their mechanisms for coping with the situation.

Background information

Friendships can be extraordinary if carefully nurtured. Good, solid friendships are an important component in a feeling of self-worth and belonging.

Choosing people to be friends with often demonstrates a person's own understanding of himself/herself; for example, people who have a positive self-image tend to attract people who also have a positive self-image; people who have low self-esteem tend to attract people who also have low self-esteem. It is important that individuals take time to get to know themselves before they can know what to look for in a friend.

In order to evaluate friendships, it is important to develop the skills involved in maintaining positive friendships. These can be listed as:

- *Talk with and listen to friends, be interested.*
- *Give positive feedback.*
- *Always use manners and be kind and considerate.*
- *Be dependable, respectful, honest and trustworthy.*
- *Help each other solve problems.*
- *Understand each other's feelings and moods.*
- *Allow for differences in opinion, giving each other the opportunity to express thoughts, feelings and ideas.*
- *Give each other room to change and grow.*

Curriculum links

England	PSHE	KS 2	Be aware of different kinds of relationships, including those between friends, and develop the skills to be effective in relationships.
Northern Ireland	PD	KS 2	Maintain positive friendships.
Republic of Ireland	SPHE	5th Class	Explore the importance of friendships and realise that making friends is part of the natural process of growing.
Scotland	Health	Level C	Show ways of making and keeping friends.
Wales	PSE	KS 2	Make and maintain friendships.

Friendships

1 You need to evaluate yourself as a person before you can establish the types of people you would like to develop friendships with.

Circle as many words as you need to in each category that you think best describe you. You can also add your own words if necessary.

My nature

loving	giving	generous
hard-working	caring	shy
happy	quiet	outgoing
trustworthy	helpful	sharing
considerate	patient	loyal
well-mannered	polite	gentle
approachable	honest	interesting
cooperative	friendly	outspoken
argumentative	thoughtful	funny
interested in others		

My interests/hobbies

watching television	computers	crafts
playing games	school	music
team sports	dancing	cooking
building models	walking	sewing
computer games	reading	writing
outdoor activities	swimming	camping
bike riding	art	nature
animals	acting	

2 Think about the qualities you would look for in a friend. You may use some of the words from above or write your own. List as many as you can in the space below.

When you meet someone for the first time, it can be a bit awkward. Both people are unsure how to behave, talk or even unsure whether you have anything in common with each other. Things need to move slowly—best friends are not made overnight!

3 So now you know what qualities you would look for in a friend. Let's say you have met a person you think has some of these qualities. How would you begin to develop a friendship?

4 Below are some steps which could be incorporated when developing a new friendship. Tick the ones you would use.

- Ask him/her about himself/herself. ☐
- Be a good listener to show that you are interested in him/her. ☐
- Be a positive person. ☐
- Be cruel and gossip about your new friend. ☐
- Share 'safe' thoughts and interests first. ☐
- Be highly opinionated and argue with everything he/she says. ☐
- Be thoughtful and helpful. ☐
- Be bossy and boastful when talking with your friend. ☐
- Spend time with him/her and get to know him/her as a person. ☐
- Expect him/her to spend all his/her time with you. ☐

Objectives

- Explores different types of relationships: child/parent, child/teacher, child/child.
- Identifies different standards of behaviour in different relationships.
- Identifies the expectations placed on him/her in different relationships.

The lesson

Discussion points:

- What is a relationship?
- Who do you have relationships with?
- What do you value about your relationships?
- Do you always act the same way in all of your relationships?
- Do different people have different expectations of you?
- What are your expectations of different people?

Materials needed/Preparation:

- A4 sheets of plain paper
- organise pupils into groups of five or six

What to do:

- Begin by discussing the first question from the Discussion points in groups. Pupils then report their ideas to the class. Pupils can then record their definition of a relationship in Question 1.
- Discuss the second question from the Discussion points. Provide pupils with paper. Ask them to draw a circle in the centre and write 'me' inside it. They then draw branches out from this circle and record all the people they have a relationship with.
- Discuss the idea that we have different relationships with different people and there may be certain things we particularly value about each relationship. Pose the question 'What do you value about your relationships?'. Pupils add this information underneath each person's name on their chart.
- Read Question 2 on the worksheet. With a partner, pupils can discuss how they act in different relationships; for example, pupils will act differently at home from when they are at school. Discuss as a class the types of words we can use to describe our behaviour and record these on the board for the pupils to refer to when completing the activity. Pupils can then complete the table using relevant keywords and phrases.
- Discuss the final two Discussion points as a whole class and emphasise that expectations go both ways; for example, teachers make expectations of pupils to have eye contact when talking, to follow the classroom rules, to be organised, to complete tasks to their best ability, to finish work on time and to use good manners. Pupils also have expectations of their teachers; for example, to be treated with respect, to learn new things, to be organised and to be helpful when they have a problem.
- Pupils can then complete Questions 3 and 4 on the worksheet.

Answers

1.–4. Answers will vary

Additional activities

- Pupils can discuss in small groups any particular problems they may have in a relationship and work together to devise possible solutions.
- Role-play in small groups scenarios of behaviour in different situations involving different relationships.
- Write a letter to a person you have a relationship with and let them know what you admire about them and what you value about your relationship.
- If you had the opportunity to change any aspect of one of your relationships, what would it be? How would you change it? Why would you want to change it?

Background information

Every day we spend time with many different people. Each person 'expects' us to behave in a different way. Our parents have expectations and so do friends, teachers, coaches and acquaintances. We are able to adjust our behaviour slightly depending on the relationship we have with a person. The way we speak with our friends is quite different from how we would speak to our teachers.

Communication is the key to developing good, strong relationships with many different people. It is important to be able to discuss issues, solve conflicts, negotiate and make decisions. We need to know how to express our thoughts and feelings but not to force them on others.

Good relationships with anyone rely on a good level of respect for each other, to be able to communicate clearly and to build a high level of trust over time.

Curriculum links

England	PSHE	KS 2	Be aware of the different kinds of relationships and develop the skills to be effective in relationships.
Northern Ireland	PD	KS 2	Maintain positive friendships and other relationships.
Republic of Ireland	SPHE	5th Class	Explore the importance of friendship and interaction with others.
Scotland	PSD		Communicate and interact within a wider circle of people.
Wales	PSE	KS 2	Make and maintain friendships and other relationships.

1 What is a relationship?

2 List keywords and phrases to describe your behaviour when you are in the company of ...

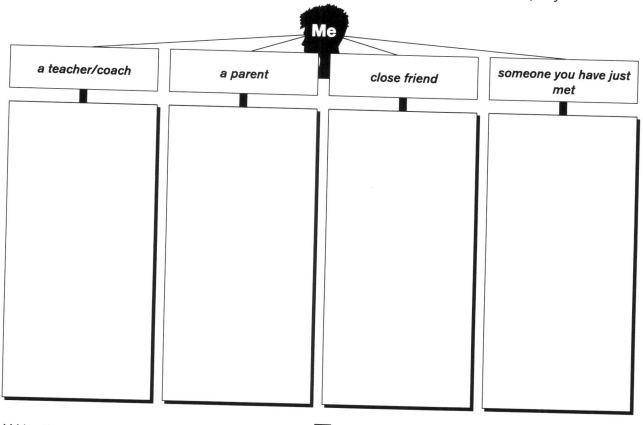

a teacher/coach	a parent	close friend	someone you have just met

3 Write the expectations placed on you by your ...

(a) *teacher.* _____

_____

_____

(b) *parent(s).* _____

_____

_____

(c) *peers.* _____

_____

_____

(d) *closest friend.* _____

_____

4 Write the expectations you place on your ...

(a) *teacher.* _____

_____

_____

(b) *parent(s).* _____

_____

_____

(c) *peers.* _____

_____

_____

(d) *closest friend.* _____

_____

Objective

• Uses conflict resolution steps to find solutions to scenarios.

The lesson

Discussion points:

• How do you cool off when you feel angry?
• What are 'I' statements? Relate some.
• What does the word 'compromise' mean?
• How can a solution be acceptable to both parties?
• What do you think is meant by a 'win-win' solution?
• What are some situations you have been in or seen where similar steps have been used?

What to do:

• Carefully read the steps and make sure the pupils understand them. Allow the pupils to read each scenario and complete their answers. Pupils who are encountering difficulty may wish to discuss the scenario with another pupil at their table. Pupils may discuss their answers as a group or as a whole class. This activity may be completed in pairs or small groups.

Answers

1.–2. Answers will vary

Additional activities

• Pupils relate scenarios they have encountered to find better solutions.
• Pupils devise then role-play conflict resolution scenarios.
• Have one pupil act as 'judge' (negotiator) to help pupils find appropriate solutions to their conflict situations. The judge is NOT to provide a solution to be enforced, but to AID in finding a solution.
• Find creative and funny solutions to everyday conflict situations. Then discuss more 'sensible' solutions.

Curriculum links

England	PSHE	KS 2	Resolve differences by looking at alternatives, making decisions and explaining choices.
Northern Ireland	PD	KS 2	Consider how challenges and issues can be avoided, lessened or resolved.
Republic of Ireland	SPHE	5th Class	Identify and discuss responses to conflict situations and how to handle conflict without being aggressive.
Scotland	PSD		Apply a problem tackling process in relevant situations.
Wales	PSE	KS 2	Develop strategies to resolve conflict.

Resolving conflicts

Conflicts frequently occur in class, in the playground and at home. Learning to deal with conflicts calmly and sensibly, using a series of established steps, provides a fair solution for both parties.

1 Read the conflict resolution steps below.

> 1. Stop and cool off.
> 2. Define the problem. (Use 'I' statements.)
>   • Tell the other person what happened
>   • Tell the other person how you feel
> 3. Brainstorm solutions.
> 4. Choose a solution that is fair to both of you. (Compromise is the key!)
> 5. Make a plan. Decide how you will put it into action.
> 6. Agree to the plan.

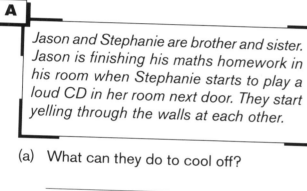

2 Use the steps to resolve the scenarios below.

A

Jason and Stephanie are brother and sister. Jason is finishing his maths homework in his room when Stephanie starts to play a loud CD in her room next door. They start yelling through the walls at each other.

(a) What can they do to cool off?

_____

_____

(b) What is the problem? _____

_____

_____

(c) What are some solutions? _____

_____

_____

(d) Which solution have you chosen?

(e) What is your plan? _____

_____

_____

(f) Have you agreed to the plan?

　█ **yes**　　**no**　█

B

Declan and Thomas are friends. They have asked to work together on a design and technology project. They don't like each other's ideas about how to complete the project. It is too late to change partners.

(a) What can they do to cool off?

_____

_____

(b) What is the problem? _____

_____

_____

(c) What are some solutions? _____

_____

_____

(d) Which solution have you chosen?

(e) What is your plan? _____

_____

_____

(f) Have you agreed to the plan?

　█ **yes**　　**no**　█

Objectives

- Identifies events that cause stress.
- Identifies activities that aid relaxation.
- Completes an action plan to combat stress.
- Recognises a simple time management strategy.

The lesson

Discussion points:

- What stresses you out?
- What makes you feel relaxed and cool about yourself?
- How does feeling good about yourself affect your day?
- How do you cope with everyday situations?
- What are your favourite forms of exercise?
- What forms of music relax you?
- Are there particular places that make you feel relaxed?

What to do:

- Discuss the points listed above. Pupils read the opening paragraph and complete Question 1.
- Read Question 2 to emphasise the steps. Discuss these to make sure that pupils fully understand them. Pupils complete Question 3 independently. Pupils may assist the teacher to create a timetable of daily class events on the board, showing times and learning areas covered, play times etc. Compare the amount of time spent completing lessons to that for relaxation.
- Read Question 4 to the pupils and allow them to attempt a time management strategy for the time after school until bedtime.

Answers

1.–4. Answers will vary since all responses are individual.

Additional activities

- Use favourite raps or rhymes as a short relaxation period between lessons. Make pupils aware of these times.
- Incorporate stretching or movement exercises to relieve stress during the day.
- Play soothing background music while the pupils are working quietly. Allow pupils to bring in appropriate choices.
- Encourage the use of a daily diary to reinforce time management skills.
- Reward good use of work time with extra free time.

Background information

Mental or emotional health is as important to maintain as physical health. Good mental health involves:

- *feeling good about yourself and your life,*
- *being able to respond constructively to stress in your life,*
- *being able to cope with events that occur in your life,*
- *self-esteem or confidence, and*
- *how you see yourself and the future.*

When you feel stressed or worried, physical reactions occur including a fast heartbeat, tense muscles, a tight stomach, feeling sick, fast breathing, sweating, difficulty sleeping or waking up still feeling tired. There are many ways to build positive mental health including doing things that you are good at and enjoy, developing personal skills to help when dealing with people, investigating new ways to cope with everyday problems, getting involved with clubs, committees, causes, helping others or occasionally taking risks and trying new things, having fun and enjoying yourself.

Curriculum links

England	PSHE	KS 2	Know what makes a healthy lifestyle and how to make informed choices.
Northern Ireland	PD	KS 2	Understand the benefits of a healthy lifestyle, including rest.
Republic of Ireland	SPHE	5th Class	Recognise and examine behaviour that is conducive to health and that which is harmful to health; e.g. balancing work and relaxation and recognise causes of personal worry and identify appropriate coping strategies.
Scotland	PSD		Take increasing responsibility for self-discipline, showing insight in planning and organising.
Wales	PSE	KS 2	Take more responsibility for keeping the body healthy and develop practical skills necessary for everyday life.

1 Complete the boxes.

At times, you may feel like everything in your life seems to be going wrong and you can't cope. You may feel tired, grumpy, anxious or confused. During these times it is difficult to think clearly and to concentrate. There are strategies to deal with stress to help you get back on track.

I feel stressed when ...	*I relax by ...*

2 When you feel stressed, you should:

- *Think about what it is that is worrying you.*
- *Talk to someone you trust about your problem.*
- *Don't agree to do any extra tasks if you really don't want to.*
- *Learn to relax.*

3 Complete the steps below to create an action plan to help you deal with stress. Use the steps from Question 2.

- I am stressed because _____

  _____

  _____

  _____

- I will talk to _____ because

  _____

  _____

  _____

- I won't be able to _____

  because _____

  _____

  _____

- I will relax by _____

  _____

  _____

  _____

4 It is easier to cope with stress if your time is managed sensibly. On a separate sheet of paper ...

- write a list of tasks that MUST be done (such as homework or projects).

- write a list of what you would LIKE to do.

- place the 'MUST DO' tasks in order of importance (or what needs to be done first).

- work out the time needed to complete them (Note: These have to be done properly!).

- do a little bit each day to make the tasks manageable.

- place some 'LIKE TO DO' activities every so often on the list to provide some relief.

• NOTE: It is better to get the MUST DO tasks done first, to give you more time for LIKE TO DO things.

Objective

• Follows decision-making steps to make a decision.

The lesson

Discussion points:

• Do you worry about what your friends will think if your decision is different from theirs?

• Do you sometimes disagree with the decisions of your friends?

• Have you ever made a decision and regretted it later? Relate some of these. (optional)

• Have you ever hurt someone by making the wrong decision?

• Have you ever made a difficult decision and been very pleased with your choice later?

• What are some things you could never do? Why would you never do them? (optional)

What to do:

• Read the opening paragraph and Question 1 with the pupils. Discuss the steps.

• Discuss the points above with the pupils before asking them to read the scenario and to answer Question 2 independently. Pupils may discuss their answers with the remainder of the class upon completion. Teachers may collect the pupils' work and read it for their own information.

Answers

1.–2. Answers will vary

> **Background information**
>
> It is important that pupils learn to stop and think about whether something is right or wrong before making a choice. The steps for decision making are:
> • define the problem,
> • brainstorm possible solutions,
> • evaluate the ideas (consider all consequences), and
> • decide on a solution and carry it out.

Additional activities

• Read other scenarios and discuss possible decisions.

• Decide who are the major decision makers at home, among your friends, at school and at your leisure groups (football club, scouts, karate club, music class etc.).

• Brainstorm a list of things or people who influence your opinions or decisions.

• Brainstorm a list of positive aspects of making a wrong decision, such as learning from experiences and hoping not to repeat the same mistakes again.

Curriculum links

England	PSHE	KS 2	Look at the alternatives, make decisions and explain choices.
Northern Ireland	PD	KS 2	Recognise the importance of decision-making.
Republic of Ireland	SPHE	5th Class	Recognise that decisions have consequences, that not all people will always make the same decisions and discuss and practise a simple decision-making strategy.
Scotland	PSD		Demonstrate their ability to select from an increasing range of choices and to discuss the reasons for the choices made.
Wales	PSE	KS 2	Develop decision-making skills.

Some decisions are easy to make, such as choosing between two types of takeaway foods, while others are more difficult. Decisions which involve a choice between right and wrong or which could have bad consequences are not easy to make.

1 Before making a difficult decision, it is important to stop and think about the results of making a particular choice. Ask yourself these questions before deciding.

- Do I feel good about this decision?

- Will I hurt someone by doing this?

- Will it be fair?

- How would I feel if someone did this to me?

- Have I been told before not to do this?

- How do I really feel about doing this, deep down?

- Will I still feel good about my decision later?

- Would the adults I respect agree with my choice?

IF YOU ARE STILL UNSURE, TALK TO SOMEONE YOU TRUST!

2 Read the scenario below and complete the decision-making questions.

Sasha and Chloe are in the 'cool' group at school. They wear the most fashionable clothes to the discos and the shopping centre. They have the latest CDs and DVDs. Their hair always looks great. They are both really good at English and maths and are very popular with the teachers and the other pupils in the class. The elections for class monitors are announced and Aimee, who is very shy, would really like to be nominated. She doesn't know whether to put her hand up to be considered because she thinks that everyone will vote for Sasha and Chloe.
What should Aimee do?

(a) What is Aimee's problem? _____
_____
_____

(b) What are her choices? _____
_____
_____
_____

(c) Look at the possible choices. Write one consequence for each of the decisions she has to make.
_____
_____
_____
_____
_____

(d) What do you think her decision should be?

Why? _____
_____
_____

Objectives

- Completes questions about empathy.
- Interviews another pupil to gain some understanding of his/her feelings, attitudes, likes and dislikes.

The lesson

Discussion points:

- How well do you know the other pupils in the class?
- Do you think that if you knew more about them, you may understand why they say, feel or do the things they do?
- How do you feel when you hear a sad or tragic news story? Do you think about how the people involved may be feeling?
- Is 'sympathy' the same as 'empathy'? Use your dictionary to find the answer.

What to do:

- Read the poem or ask an individual pupil to read it to the class. Discuss the poem, ensuring that pupils fully understand what it is about. Pupils complete Questions 2 to 4. A dictionary is needed to answer Question 2.
- Pupils form pairs to complete Questions 5 and 6. It is best to form pairs from pupils who don't know each other well. Pupils may share their answers to Questions 1 to 4 with the class and discuss answers. Interview sheets may be shown to the teacher if given permission by the pupil who was interviewed.

Answers

1.–6. Answers will vary

Additional activities

- Read scenarios about how pupils may feel in different situations. Would you feel the same?
- Recall some sad news stories such as the bombings in Bali. Did you feel sorry for families who lost brothers, sisters, mothers, fathers, sons and daughters? Can you imagine how it would feel if someone in your family had been hurt or killed there?
- Allow pupils to relate good things that have happened to them. Sometimes good news must be shared immediately.
- Allow talking and listening times within the class, with a one- or two-minute time limit, for pupils to share news with others.
- Choose a pupil of the week. Pupils prepare and display a biography about themselves.

Background information

Empathy means 'mentally entering into the feeling or spirit of a person or thing'. Simply speaking, 'empathy' means to feel sympathetic towards another person or to be in accord with him/her. For children this means putting themselves in someone else's place and imagining how that person feels. Pupils need to be appreciative and tolerant of differences in others. It is sometimes easier to ridicule the unknown or unfamiliar than to show sympathy and understanding.

Curriculum links

England	PSHE	KS 2	Care about other people's feelings.
Northern Ireland	PD	KS 2	Be sensitive towards others.
Republic of Ireland	SPHE	5th Class	Express and cope with feelings in an appropriate manner; e.g. empathise with the feelings of others.
Scotland	PSD		Demonstrate respect and tolerance towards others.
Wales	PSE	KS 2	Empathise with others' experiences and feelings.

1 (a) Read the poem below.

> If I had to walk in your shoes
>
> My socks would slip and my heels would bruise.
>
> Your shoes are too big and mine are too small
>
> Can we really understand each other at all?
>
> Wouldn't it be great; wouldn't it be cool
>
> To follow this golden rule!
>
> 'If you want to know how another person feels
>
> Put yourself in their place' (but mind the heels!)

(b) What is the poem about?

_____

_____

_____

_____

2 Look up the word 'empathy' in a dictionary and write the meaning.

_____

_____

_____

3 Why is it important to be able to put yourself in someone else's place?

_____

_____

_____

_____

4 Give an example of a time when you really wanted to know how another person was feeling.

_____

_____

_____

_____

_____

_____

_____

Learning about another person helps us to understand how they are feeling and why they do things. We learn to accept and appreciate their similarities and differences.

5 Choose a pupil in your class who you don't know very well. Interview the pupil and complete the questions below.

(a) What are the things you like the most?

(b) What are the things you dislike the most?

(c) What is the worst thing that has happened to you?

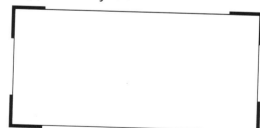

(d) What is the best thing that has happened to you?

6 Read your report to the pupil who was interviewed to see whether you recorded the information correctly. Do not share this information with anyone else unless you are given permission from the pupil who was interviewed.

Objective

• Identifies factors which make up a healthy or unhealthy lifestyle.

The lesson

Discussion points:

• What do you think it means to have an unhealthy lifestyle?
• What do you think it means to have a healthy lifestyle?
• What are the benefits/advantages of a healthy lifestyle?
• Does a healthy lifestyle only include active activities?
• How would you rate your own lifestyle?
• How could you improve your lifestyle?

What to do:

• Ask two pupils to read the recipe for an unhealthy lifestyle. One could read the ingredients and one the method or the pupils can take turns in reading one ingredient at a time. Encourage a humorous tone and allow laughter!

• Pupils can suggest other unhealthy ingredients and methods. List these on the blackboard/whiteboard. Pupils can choose from these or add their own to complete Question 1.

• Question 1 will lead pupils into thinking about what is healthy in order to decide what is unhealthy. Use some of the discussion points to prepare pupils to complete the healthy recipe in Question 2. Pupils could work in pairs.

• Share recipes when complete.

• Allow pupils to contemplate their own lifestyles and give themselves a rating out of 10.

• Individually, or after a discussion with a partner, complete Question 4. Share responses.

Answers

1.–4. Teacher check

Background information

A healthy lifestyle is active and well-balanced in terms of physical activity, healthy eating, relaxation, sleep and personal hygiene. The benefits of a healthy lifestyle include weight control, a healthier heart, improved lung capacity, clearer skin, good muscle tone, healthy teeth, better sleep patterns, a sense of wellbeing, improved self-esteem and more energy.

Additional activities

• Pupils create their own recipes for healthy and unhealthy lifestyles. Display on a pin-up board or compile into two class books.

• Collate pupils' ratings of their lifestyles (do this anonymously to save embarrassment) and discuss how healthy the class is on average.

• Brainstorm lists of ideas for a healthy lifestyle and display on a chart as a checklist.

Curriculum links

England	PSHE	KS 2	Know what makes a healthy lifestyle.
Northern Ireland	PD	KS 2	Understand the benefits of a healthy lifestyle.
Republic of Ireland	SPHE	5th Class	Recognise and examine behaviour that is conducive and harmful to health.
Scotland	Health	Level D	Show their knowledge and understanding of their physical needs.
Wales	PSE	KS 2	Take more responsibility for keeping the body healthy.

1 Read the recipe below for an unhealthy lifestyle. Add another unhealthy ingredient and method of your own.

Ingredients

- 2 kg of junk food
- many hours of television
- 3 computer games
- 1 L soft drink
- lots of stale air
- 5 mins sunshine
- 5 mins exercise
- shallow breathing
- 5 late nights
- _____
  _____

Method

1. Divide the junk food into sections to eat throughout the day. Do the same with the soft drink. (Optional: Guzzle in one session and eat and drink more later in the day.)
2. Play the computer games continuously in a stuffy room full of stale air.
3. Allow 5 mins only of sunshine and exercise when walking slowly to put junk food containers in the bin.
4. Shallow breathe while watching television until late 5 nights a week.
5. _____
   _____

2 Make up a recipe for a healthy lifestyle. Add a suitable illustration if you wish.

Ingredients

Method

3 Think about your own lifestyle. Which recipe is it like (or is it a mixture of both)? Rate your own lifestyle on this scale (10 being the best).

1	2	3	4	5	6	7	8	9	10

4 How could you improve your recipe for a healthy lifestyle? List your suggestions under 'Ingredients' and 'Method' below.

Ingredients	Method

Objectives

- Understands the meaning of values.
- Identifies some of his/her own values.

The lesson

Discussion points:

- What do you think a value is?
- What kinds of things do you value?
- 'Sometimes not knowing what our values are can lead us to do things we don't really want to do.' Discuss.

Materials needed/Preparation:

- The day before the lesson, ask pupils to think about who their heroes are and who they admire. Ask the class to bring in some information and (if possible) pictures of that person for the following health lesson. This may require pupils to have access to the school's computers to download information from the Internet. (Be aware of which personalities they have chosen before giving them access to the Internet.)

What to do:

- Pupils complete Questions 1 and 2 independently. Ask pupils to volunteer to read their responses to the class.
- Discuss with the pupils that it is important to think about what we value. We can often have our values challenged by our peers and so we need to feel confident about our values.
- Pupils complete an 'email' to a penfriend describing themselves, their interests and their values. Explain that this piece of writing is personal and does not have to be shared with the class. Some pupils may wish to volunteer to read their emails to the class. Discuss what values the email is expressing.

Answers

1.–3. Answers will vary

Background information

Our values create the basis for how we lead our lives. When we have confidence in ourselves and strong values, it is easier to do things that are right for us. Those who have weaker values can often be easily led and may end up doing things they don't really want to do.

Teachers can discuss some values with pupils such as honesty, generosity, tolerance and kindness. They may also like to discuss other things people may value like pets, music and the environment.

Additional activities

- Pupils choose a style of poetry and write a poem to express what they value. Options could include an acrostic poem, a shape poem or a rhyming poem.
- Write a narrative involving a group of four pupils. One of the pupils has his/her values challenged by the other group members. Does he/she give in and follow the group or does he/she stand up for his/her values and ignore the group?

  The story must have a beginning, middle and end and have a well-defined central character.
- Pupils present a polished piece of poetry or narrative text on coloured card for display.

Curriculum links

England	PSHE	KS 2	Talk and write about their own opinions and explain their views.
Northern Ireland	PD	KS 2	Know how to confidently express their own views and opinions.
Republic of Ireland	SPHE	5th Class	Express personal opinions, thoughts and ideas.
Scotland	PSD		Identify their own values and attitudes.
Wales	PSE	KS 2	Be confident in their own values.

1 Do you have a hero or someone who you admire and would like to be like? Who is it and what is it about that person that you admire? Write about your hero below and either find and glue or sketch a picture of him/her in the box.

2 Think about your friends. What is it about them that you like and admire? Do they have any similar qualities? Complete the sentence.

The qualities my friends have include: _____

_____

_____

_____

**Remember that your values are what you consider to be important in life.
Sometimes it can be hard to know what we value.
By completing these activities, you are helping to identify your values.**

3 Your teacher has just returned from a holiday to the USA where she visited a local primary school and swapped email addresses with the Year 6 teacher there. You have been allocated a pupil from the class to correspond with and must now create an email telling him/her about yourself. Include in your email:

your interests   *your goals (career and others)*   *what is important to you*

To:

From: **Send**

Subject:

Objective

• Identifies and describes tolerant and intolerant behaviour.

The lesson

Discussion points:

• What does the word 'tolerance' mean?

• Describe tolerant behaviours.

• Describe intolerant behaviours.

• Why do you think people show intolerant behaviour towards others? (ignorance, jealousy, impatience etc.)

What to do:

• Explain to the class that they are going to be writing a story in this lesson. The story will be about a new boy joining a class.

• Read the text at the top of the page. Discuss with the class what it might be like to join a new class. On the board, write a list of words to describe how the pupil might be feeling.

• Now ask the class what they think it would be like to join a new class when you are still grasping the language. Add to the list on the board.

• If there are pupils in the class who have experienced the above, ask them if they would like to share their experiences.

• Pupils can work in groups to discuss the kinds of behaviour the four pupils in the story will be exhibiting.

• Pupils work independently to plan and then write their stories. Some pupils may need guidance with their writing.

• Ask pupils to share their stories with the class.

Answers

1.–2. Answers will vary

Additional activities

• Pupils can role-play their story with other members of the class.

• Hold a discussion on how the class reacts or would react to a new person joining. Be sensitive not to use names.

• Make a class list of tolerant behaviour that can be shown toward each other, the teacher and other staff and pupils in the school. Display the list in the classroom.

• When the narrative texts are at the polished stage, pupils could publish them on the computer and print them out. Collate the stories to make a class book that can be added to the class library and read during silent reading times.

Background information

We live in a multicultural society. We look different. We live differently. Differences can enhance our relationships and enrich our society. Pupils need to be taught to recognise, appreciate and tolerate differences.

Tolerance is a skill which can reduce conflict. It is an ongoing process.

Teaching tolerance is also teaching pupils not to hate. Teachers can teach tolerance most effectively by modelling tolerant behaviour in the classroom and the playground. Pupils should be exposed to people, literature and images that are multicultural and which teach them about other faiths, ethnicities and lifestyles.

Educating pupils to be tolerant will:

• *promote the understanding and acceptance of people with individual differences.*

• *minimise generalisations and stereotyping.*

• *help pupils to understand and appreciate the differences between people.*

• *highlight the need to combat prejudice and discrimination.*

Curriculum links

England	PSHE	KS 2	Care about other people's feelings.
Northern Ireland	PD	KS 2	Be sensitive towards others.
Republic of Ireland	SPHE	5th Class	Recognise the importance of care, consideration and courtesy when dealing with others.
Scotland	PSD		Demonstrate respect and tolerance towards others.
Wales	PSE	KS 2	Show care and consideration for others.

The pupils in class 6R have been together since they were 5-years-old. They know most things about each other and have shared lots of memories. Mrs Riddle tells them that as of Monday a new boy will be joining the class. Antonio is from Spain and he has only been learning English for the last few years. Mrs Riddle tells her class that she expects them to show kindness, understanding and tolerance toward Antonio.

Write a narrative that describes how 6R reacted to Antonio on his first day. Include six main characters: Mrs Riddle, Antonio, two pupils who do not show tolerance toward Antonio and two pupils who are kind toward him. Resolve the situation in the last paragraph.

1 Plan your narrative text below.

Title: _____

Characters: **Mrs Riddle**   **Antonio**

Pupil 1: _____   Character type: _____

Pupil 2: _____   Character type: _____

Pupil 3: _____   Character type: _____

Pupil 4: _____   Character type: _____

Setting: The classroom of 6R and _____

_____

Beginning:

Middle:

End:

2 Use your plan to write the first draft of your narrative on the back of this sheet.
Ask a friend to read and comment on your story before you begin the second draft.

Objectives

- Recognises actions that are disrespectful.
- Considers ways to act respectfully toward others.
- Identifies ways of showing respect to other people.

The lesson

Discussion points:

- What does 'respect' mean?
- Who do you respect the most? Why?
- Who shows you respect?
- 'It is important that we respect ourselves.' Discuss.

What to do:

- Divide the class into small groups. The groups discuss each scenario.
  They can discuss: Who is being disrespectful?
  Who is not being respected?
  How are they not being respected?
- In groups or independently, the pupils write ways they can show respect to the people in their lives.
- Discuss with the class why it is important to have self-respect. Explain that we should all treat others the way we expect to be treated ourselves.
- Independently, the pupils complete Question 2. Ask the pupils who need guidance to think about the following:
  – How do you like to be spoken to?
  – Do you expect people to act fairly towards you?
  – Do you expect people to tell you the truth?

Answers

1.–2. Answers will vary

Background information

Treating others with respect makes the world a nicer place. We show respect to others when we treat them the way we would like to be treated.

A respectful person:
- *is courteous and polite,*
- *listens to what others have to say,*
- *doesn't insult, judge or make fun of people, call them names or bully them,*
- *doesn't judge people before he/she gets to know them,*
- *is sensitive to the feelings of others, and*
- *doesn't put pressure on someone to do something he/she doesn't want to do.*

Additional activities

- Pupils discuss each scenario and decide what they think the consequence for each behaviour should be. Ask the groups to share their responses with the class. Are there discrepancies between the level of punishment? Why? Discuss.
- Pupils can role-play some of the scenarios on the worksheet. They can then perform role-plays where the person not being respectfully treated confronts the other person and asks why they are acting the way they are.
- In groups, pupils create posters with the heading RESPECT! They can use text, pictures, art materials etc. to present their own visions of what respect means to them.

Curriculum links

England	PSHE	KS 2	Care about other people's feelings and try to see things from their point of view.
Northern Ireland	PD	KS 2	Develop self-respect and have respect for rules, property, the law and authority.
Republic of Ireland	SPHE	5th Class	Recognise the importance of care, consideration and courtesy when dealing with others and respect others' beliefs, views and opinions.
Scotland	PSD		Demonstrate respect towards others.
Wales	PSE	KS 2	Respect others and their property.

1 Read each scenario. Discuss it with your group. Consider how you can act respectfully toward the people in your life. Write your ideas in each box.

Jason comes home from school in a bad mood. He walks into the house, drops his bag in the middle of the hall and walks to the fridge. He ignores his mum who asks him how his day was. He takes a snack from the fridge, walks to his room and shuts the door.	I can respect my family by ….
Three boys are sitting at the back of the bus. They use marker pens to draw on the back of the seats and on the wall. The bus driver cannot see what they are doing.	I can respect my community by …
Lizzy is at her grandma's 70th birthday party. She has her CD Walkman® with her and listens to her music for most of the day. Some of her grandma's friends try to speak to her but Lizzy just shouts 'What?' at them.	I can respect the elderly by …
Nanthini tells her friend, Sophie, something in confidence. A few days later, Nanthini hears a few other girls from her class whispering about her and laughing.	I can respect my friends by …
Philip thought he was playing an amazing game of football until the coach asked him to come off. Philip was furious as he walked towards the bench and yelled at his coach that he needed glasses.	I can respect my coach/teacher by …

Showing respect for yourself and others is an important quality to develop.
We show respect for others when we treat them the way we like to be treated ourselves.

2 Describe how you expect to be treated by others. _____

_____

_____

_____

Objectives

- Generates personal goals which are based on being fit and active.
- Devises strategies to attain his/her personal goals.
- Evaluates his/her decisions in the process of setting personal goals.

The lesson

Discussion points:

- What is a goal?
- Do you ever set goals for yourself?
- Do you always achieve your goals?
- How do you feel when you achieve your goals? How do you feel when you don't achieve your goals?
- What is your definition of success?
- 'It is okay to set lower goals than to risk failure by setting higher ones.' Agree or disagree?

Materials needed/Preparation:

- organise pupils into groups of five or six

What to do:

- Begin by discussing the first question from the Discussion points in groups. Pupils then report their ideas about what a goal is to the class.
- Direct pupils to the worksheet and read through the Steps for Goal Setting. Talk about each point and ask pupils to contribute their own examples of goal setting.
- Discuss questions two and three from the Discussion points in small groups. Spend a short period of time with each group to gather an idea of who sets goals and who doesn't. As a whole class, talk about the importance of setting goals in order to be successful (see Background information).
- As a class, brainstorm some goals pupils may like to set; for example, in health and fitness, the arts or spelling or developing new friendships and being more organised. Remember it must be expressed in terms which can be measured. Establish which goals would be long-term or short-term.
- Discuss questions four and five from the Discussion points. Record pupils' answers on the board using keywords and phrases. Develop a class definition for success. This could be presented on a chart and used to motivate pupils on a daily basis.
- Direct pupils to complete the table in Question 1 on the worksheet. Encourage pupils to select one short-term and one long-term goal.
- Discuss or debate the final statement from the Discussion points in small groups.
- Each pupil can then complete Question 2 by evaluating his/her decisions and modify his/her goals as required.

Answers

1.–2. Answers will vary

Additional activities

- Pupils can periodically check their goals to ensure they are on target for meeting them.
- Set some class goals that will encourage pupils to work together for a common purpose.
- Practise setting short-term and long-term goals on a regular basis. Evaluate pupils' success rates.
- Present the class's definition of 'success' on a large, bright chart as a motivational tool.
- Display class goals on a large chart near the 'success' chart in order to keep the class on target.

Background information

People who experience success set goals. They formulate their goals and set into motion a strategy to help them meet their goal within a set time. Those who are successful often have a mentor they report to on a regular basis who helps to keep them on track. Successful people:

- *have a clear vision of what they want and where they wish to be in life.*
- *develop a clear strategy which states how, when and what they need to do.*
- *experience passion for their goal. They are excited about it!*
- *are honest with themselves about what they need to do and about their strengths and weaknesses.*
- *are flexible.*
- *take risks or move outside the area where they feel most comfortable.*
- *surround themselves with people who want them to be successful.*
- *put goals into action and achieve them.*
- *prioritise goals and actions that need to be achieved.*
- *manage their own mental, physical, emotional and spiritual self.*

Curriculum links

England	PSHE	KS 2	Set personal goals.
Northern Ireland	PD	KS 2	Set goals for improvement.
Republic of Ireland	SPHE	5th Class	Identify realistic goals and targets and the strategies required to reach these.
Scotland	PSD		Set realistic goals.
Wales	PSE	KS 2	Set targets for improvement.

Steps for Goal Setting

1. What is your goal? Write it clearly.
2. When do you want to achieve your goal? Set a target date.
3. How will you work toward achieving your goal? Plan a step-by-step strategy.
4. Who will help you achieve your goal? Arrange to have a mentor.
5. Why is this goal so important to you? Consider why you want to achieve it.

1 Set yourself two goals.

	Goal 1	Goal 2
Goal		
Target date		
Strategy		
Possible obstacles		
Mentor		
How will I know when I have achieved my goal?		
This goal is important to me because ...		

2 Evaluate your decisions in setting your personal goals.

(a) I set realistic goals.

1	2	3	4	5	6	7	8	9	10

(b) I set realistic time lines.

1	2	3	4	5	6	7	8	9	10

(c) My strategies are clearly laid out for me to follow.

1	2	3	4	5	6	7	8	9	10

(d) I have included approaches to solve any problems that may occur.

1	2	3	4	5	6	7	8	9	10

(e) I have selected a mentor whom I trust to help me.

1	2	3	4	5	6	7	8	9	10

Objectives

- Understands that commitment to a project is part of being responsible.
- Considers carefully a project he/she would like to participate in and plans his/her involvement in detail.

The lesson

Discussion points:

- What does it mean to be 'responsible'?
- What are the benefits of being responsible?
- Do you think people are responsible when it comes to the environment?
- Why does commitment play such a big part in being responsible?
- Do you think the level of importance of something plays a part in how much energy you put into a project? Explain.

Materials needed/Preparation:

- organise pupils into groups of five or six.
- paper for each group.
- Internet, telephone directories, telephone, local maps.

What to do:

- Begin by developing an understanding about what it is to be responsible. Organise the class into small groups and give each group a piece of paper for recording the group's responses to the first discussion question.
- Ask pupils to consider the benefits of being responsible, such as freedom, self-respect, decision making, increases self-esteem etc. Share these ideas with the whole class.
- Read the Background information to the pupils and discuss the third question from the Discussion points. Pupils will have varying ideas on this topic, depending on whether or not they are involved in groups which are environmentally aware or whether or not they are environmentally aware themselves.
- Direct pupils to the worksheet. Explain to the pupils that this activity requires them to carefully consider an environmental project in their local area pertaining to the care and recovery of local waterways. If your local environment does not lend itself to this topic, a study of water use in the home and school could be undertaken.
- Pupils complete Questions 1 to 5 on the worksheet. Pupils can access the Internet or telephone services to make contact with organisations in order to fully research the project he/she might like to participate in. Ensure pupils have adequate practice at gathering information over the telephone (polite introduction, explanation of the project and appropriate questions to ask, polite salutation).
- Discuss, as a whole class, the final two questions from the Discussion points. Ensure pupils have an understanding of the importance of being committed to a project (turning up on time, maintaining enthusiasm etc.) as a group comes to depend and rely on you.
- Pupils can then complete the remainder of the worksheet.

Answers

1.–10. Answers will vary

Additional activities

- Follow through with the project and encourage pupils to report their experiences to the class via photographs, talks, posters, charts, guest speakers and so on.
- Pupils can keep a diary of their thoughts and feelings and how they feel the experience has helped them as a person.
- Pupils can collaborate on an environmental project within the school. They need to write a directive, including what they intend to do, the time they will be able to dedicate to the project, who will help them with the project, the outcome they wish to achieve and by when it is to be achieved.

Background information

Concern regarding our waterways has increased and people are becoming more aware of the problems facing our waterways. The media regularly present the public with new information on how they can help to protect the water quality of our rivers, streams, lakes and ponds. A number of initiatives have been put in place for the general public, school pupils and organisations to become involved in programmes which range from testing water quality to recording wildlife found in particular locations to clearing rubbish out of rivers and lakes. These groups monitor their waterways and over time can establish whether the environmental quality of the waterway is improving, declining or being maintained. Many groups have successfully implemented new projects such as fencing areas of riverbanks, eradicating weeds and reducing the use of pesticides and other pollutants to improve the quality of their local waterways.

See the Internet:
http://www.environment-agency.gov.uk

http://www.britishwaterways.co.uk

http://www.defra.gov.uk/environment/water

http://www.waterwaysireland.org

Curriculum links

England	PSHE	KS 2	Recognise the role of voluntary and community groups and realise how economic choices affect the sustainability of the environment.
Northern Ireland	PD	KS 2	Play an active and meaningful part in the life of the community and be concerned about the wider environment.
Republic of Ireland	SPHE	5th Class	Appreciate the environment and develop a sense of community responsibility for caring for the environment.
Scotland	Health	Level D	Identify ways in which the wider community takes action to protect health.
Wales	PSE	KS 2	Take an active interest in the life of the community and be concerned about the wider environment.

Looking after your environment means being responsible.

1 Think about and decide what you would like to do to improve your local waterways.

2 How can you find out more information about what you would like to do? (Use resources.)

3 Is there a suitable project already running? ■ yes ___ no ■

4
Name of project: _____   Who runs it: _____

Telephone: _____   Email: _____

Where: _____   When: _____

What: _____
_____
_____

5 What will be your role in the project?

6 How much time will you dedicate to the project? (Be specific about hours and days each week or month. Also consider other commitments you already have.)

My time:

School time:

7 How do you plan to follow through with your commitment?

8 How long do you plan to work on this project?

9 Are you going to do this project ...

■ **independently?** ___   ■ **with friends?** ■

■ **with family?**   ■ **as a class?** ■

10 Explain why this project is important to you and how you will feel by participating.

_____
_____